Legacy
of a
Lifetime

Legacy *of a* Lifetime

A PLANNED GIVING IMPLEMENTATION RESOURCE

Robert L. Sessum and
L. Pendleton Armistead

CHURCH
PUBLISHING
INCORPORATED

Copyright © 2021 by Robert L. Sessum and L. Pendleton Armistead

All rights reserved. No part of this book may be reproduced, stored in a retrieval system, or transmitted in any form or by any means, electronic or mechanical, including photocopying, recording, or otherwise, without the written permission of the publisher.

Downloadable supplemental material can be found at https://www.churchpublishing.org/legacyofalifetime.

Church Publishing
19 East 34th Street
New York, NY 10016
www.churchpublishing.org

Cover design by Gillian Whiting
Interior design and typesetting by Beth Oberholtzer

Library of Congress Cataloging-in-Publication Data

Names: Sessum, Robert L., author. | Armistead, L. Pendleton, author.
Title: Legacy of a lifetime : a planned giving implementation resource / Robert L. Sessum and L. Pendleton Armistead.
Description: New York : Church Publishing, [2021]
Identifiers: LCCN 2020054772 (print) | LCCN 2020054773 (ebook) | ISBN 9781640653801 (paperback) | ISBN 9781640653818 (epub)
Subjects: LCSH: Church fund raising. | Deferred giving—Religious aspects—Christianity.
Classification: LCC BV772.5 .S47 2021 (print) | LCC BV772.5 (ebook) | DDC 248/.6—dc23
LC record available at https://lccn.loc.gov/2020054772
LC ebook record available at https://lccn.loc.gov/2020054773

*This book is dedicated to the members of the
Society of the Good Shepherd who, through their
expressions of generosity and commitment of faith, will have
a lasting impact on their parish and will continue the works
of our Heavenly Father for generations to come.*

Contents

Acknowledgments	ix
Introduction: Six Components of Successful Giving	xi
The Cycle of Giving	xix
Master Documents	**1**
Master Schedule	3
Plan of Campaign	5
Organizational Structure	15
Solicitation Process	17
Month by Month	**21**
Month 1 Preparation, Prospect Research, and Cultivation	23
Month 2 Planning and Prospect Research	31
Month 3 Preparation, Prospect Research, and Cultivation	45
Month 4 Planning, Prospect Research, and Cultivation	59
Month 5 Planning, Prospect Research, Cultivation, and Solicitation	77
Month 6 Planning, Prospect Research, Cultivation, and Solicitation	89
Month 7 Prospect Research, Cultivation, and Solicitation	101
Month 8 Prospect Research, Cultivation, and Solicitation	113
Month 9 Prospect Research, Cultivation, and Solicitation	127
Month 10 Prospect Research, Cultivation, and Solicitation	141
Month 11 Cultivation and Solicitation	153
Month 12 Cultivation and Solicitation	165
Conclusion	**175**

Acknowledgments

Since this model program was designed and implemented successfully at the Episcopal Church of the Good Shepherd in Lexington, Kentucky, the authors wish to express acknowledgment and appreciation to the vestry and staff, the task force, the members of the congregation, and the volunteers and donors. Through their diligence, perseverance, and sacrifice, a significant achievement was realized. The overall outcome was an expression and reaffirmation of the congregation to proclaim the grace and glory of God and advance God's will.

God's Peace,
Robert L. Sessum, MDiv   L. Pendleton Armistead, EdD

INTRODUCTION
Six Components of Successful Giving

The decision for a church to move into a planned gifts program is an important one, with major implications and an equal number of opportunities. Clearly, this effort can have a profound and lasting impact on a church's ability to secure significant funding in support of its vision. However, to achieve the overarching goals, this program should be viewed as a systemic effort that is well organized, formalized, and supported by the clergy, governing board, and members associated with its stewardship program. When implemented in this manner, the church will experience a wide array of benefits that go beyond just realizing significant financial resources.

This planned gifts program, which is intended to be congregation-wide, provides a forum for disseminating information on a church's long-range goals. These goals may include advancement of various programs and services, capital development projects, or endowment building. Through implementation of a planned gifts program, a sense of community and ownership are created. By acquiring the perceptions and attitudes of worshippers, participants will become more vested in the process and the desired outcomes. If an individual or couple decides to include the church in their estate planning, it is an indication and validation of a long-term commitment to the church.

This program promotes a culture of giving. In most instances, congregations provide support to their church by way of the annual stewardship program. While this venue is important for the daily operation of the church, it rarely accommodates additional resources to promote growth and advancement of important long-term initiatives. Through personal financial sacrifice and the sharing of God's gifts for the benefit of others, members of the congregation realize a greater sense of fulfillment.

While this program is provided for planned giving, it certainly can be used for targeted major fundraising: capital campaigns, strategic projects, as well as endowment goals. The tools can be adjusted depending on the situation.

The starting point for effective implementation is to integrate broad-based and proven parameters that serve as cornerstones for the planned gifts program. These essential components can be categorized into six tenets:

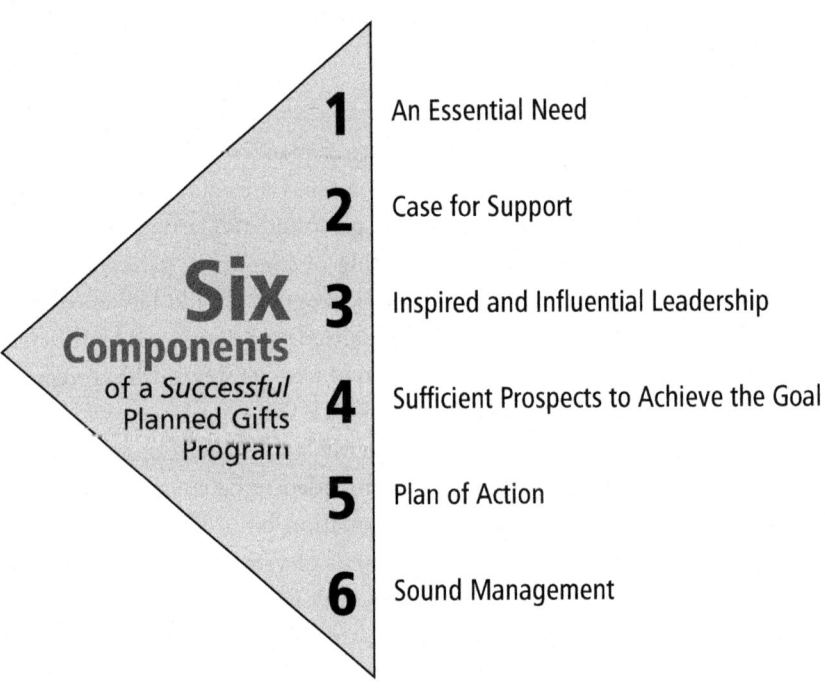

Six Components of a *Successful* Planned Gifts Program

1. An Essential Need
2. Case for Support
3. Inspired and Influential Leadership
4. Sufficient Prospects to Achieve the Goal
5. Plan of Action
6. Sound Management

1. An Essential Need

The church must have a clear vision of its future—a future that creates new or improved benefits for its congregations. The church must prioritize and quantify its needs as expressed in the strategic, master, and operational planning vehicles. The various components of the "vision" provide the impetus for developing and determining fundraising goals for both the laypeople and community in which the church serves—over short, intermediate, and long-range timeframes.

More specifically, the essential need should:

- Be aggressive, yet attainable, with given benchmarks and short, intermediate, and long-term objectives.
- Provide the impetus for desired and sustainable growth.
- Determine fundraising goals specific to project church-based needs.
- Specify new or improved benefits for constituencies.

Some relevant questions to address include:

- Does the church have a strategic vision?
- Are the mission, vision, and value statements clearly defined?
- Was there broad-based participation in creating the plan?
- Are the financial requirements of the plan quantified and project specific?
- Is the church maximizing all existing funding sources to meet its needs?
- Can the church prove it is cost effective?
- Have the financial requirements of the church been shared with stakeholders?
- Were fundraising goals determined by the strategic vision?

2. Case for Support

The church must be able to express clearly the benefits it provides and to whom. It must establish a unique identity in terms of distinct competencies and strengths. The "Case for Support" defines the church's mission, goals, and natural constituencies, and the benefits it provides to these groups. In this regard, an effective "Case for Support" is also a marketing statement. The church's benefits are communicated in a manner that prompts a positive response on the part of prospective donors.

The "Case for Support" should:

- Establish a unique identity.
- Define competencies.
- Define mission, vision, goals, and constituencies.
- Become the basis of promoting awareness and marketing.

Specific determinations of the following questions should be undertaken as related to the scope and context of the "Case for Support":

- Does the church have a compelling "Case for Support"?
- Are the church's financial needs unique and clearly discerned?
- Does the church know its strengths and challenges?
- Does the church have a marketing and awareness plan?
- Is resource development considered a church-wide priority?
- Is the church leadership constantly advocating the church's causes in the congregation and beyond?
- In comparison to other community needs, are the church's requirements considered significant by key church leaders?

3. Inspired and Influential Leadership

The church's ability to raise financial support is directly related to the quality of leadership recruited and trained for this purpose. Further, success is equally related to the extent to which this leadership has assisted in shaping and defining how the church can become stronger and of greater value to those it serves. Demographic characteristics, leadership representation, geographic reach and church-wide involvement, as well as diversity of representation, are essential.

In essence, effective leadership should:

- Be composed of top-quality members based upon influence and affluence.
- Be dedicated to and involved in the life of the church.
- Be engaged in significant peer-to-peer interactions and relationships throughout the entire church community.

Further, since the planned gifts program is dependent upon the effective use of volunteers, review of the following questions is beneficial:

- Has the church educated top leadership on the mission, role, and achievements of the church?
- Can the effort engage top-quality members based on influence and affluence?
- Does the church's stewardship program involve a broad base of its constituency?
- Has the church been asking a broad base of the church's constituency to give?
- Has the time of volunteers been used wisely and well?

4. Sufficient Prospects to Achieve the Goal

The research function identifies individuals that have a philosophical rationale for becoming involved in the life of the church and have the potential to make initial and significant gifts. It also specifies the most effective way to cultivate and solicit planned gifts from these sources, and is the continuing source of strategic information for all stewardship functions.

The research function is essential to identifying potential sources of support and engagement, and allows for documentation of the need and impact of the proposed program. This function is based on the premise that a prospective donor is likely to contribute if the church demonstrates that, through its strengths, it offers a capacity to address opportunities the prospect considers worthwhile. Donors want to feel they are investing in something they care about—something that offers a real and observable change. An effective research component is based on this marketing perspective.

Effective prospect research programs:

- Identify and align individuals with a philosophical rationale for involvement.
- Define strategies of awareness and cultivation as a means of maximizing gift potential.
- Provide strategic direction in ensuring a realistic pipeline of prospects interested in creating systemic and sustainable growth.

As a means of gauging the possibility of securing planned gifts, a review of the following questions is warranted:

- Does the church have a research component that is constantly identifying potential significant donors?
- Can the church identify worshippers with the qualities of influence and/or affluence?
- Is the church aware of how many individuals of affluence are active and engaged with the church?
- Has the church identified a sufficient number of affluent individuals to achieve the church's vision?

5. Plan of Action

The plan of action is a blueprint to achieve specific fundraising goals that support the church's vision of its future. The plan includes a schedule to carry out the strategies identified through the research component and offers a coordinated direction that has measures and benchmarks for accountability. It communicates to volunteers that the planned gifts program is well organized, and will result in specific and defined levels of change, growth, and success.

The plan of action or "plan for growth and development" should:

- Be a comprehensive, broad-based, and coordinated approach to resolving church and/or community-based needs.
- Reflect the philosophies supporting the uniqueness of the church.
- Promote and achieve success by matching quality volunteers with prospective donors.

The "plan of action" is a detailed strategy for employment of a planned gifts campaign. It is designed to build upon the strengths of the church, limit the challenges, and create significant opportunities that are unique to the individual church. The plan is the tool by which accountability measures are assessed and the realized outcomes are determined. The following questions are consistent with this component:

- Does the church (governing board) have a strategic plan of action?
- Has the plan been shared with top leadership?

- Do key leaders believe the plan is likely to succeed?
- Does the plan include specific fundraising goals and initiatives?
- Does the church have a schedule for achieving the goals outlined in its plan?
- Is the plan based upon tested principles and experience?
- Has the plan been reviewed and adjusted on a regular basis?

6. Sound Management

Since effective fundraising programs rely heavily on the participation of enthusiastic volunteers of influence and affluence, it follows that a management component must also stimulate, coordinate, and sustain volunteer activities. A centralized function is mandatory. The planned gifts "campaign manager" handles the management of the volunteer resources and the fundraising program—in coordination and frequent communication with the stewardship body. Further, participation of the church's administrator is essential. The extent of success of the fundraising program is tied to the effectiveness of this management structure.

The concept of sound management is embodied in the fact that all entities associated with stewardship are acting as one cohesive unit, working in a common and unified direction. Further, sound management assumes:

- The church's governing board, stewardship committee, and clergy are supportive, and promote the goals and objectives of the church.
- It is aligned with the organizational structure of the church.
- It incorporates and reflects auxiliary functions of the church.

Critical to the level of success of the endeavor is the church's ability to sustain the promotion and subsequent acquisition of planned gifts on an ongoing basis. In order to fully realize the benefits of the program, constancy and continuation are important. Promotion of the program is based upon awareness and cultivation. Acquisition of gifts is dependent upon volunteer structures and solicitation processes. As such, a commitment of necessary financial and human resources is required—from clergy, governing board, and the stewardship body. Review of the following items will assist the church to determine if an appropriate level of commitment exists to sustain the planned gifts program—from a management perspective:

- Is the planned gifts program of genuine interest to the clergy?
- Is the governing board willing to allocate appropriate levels of funding on an annual basis?
- Can the stewardship committee serve as the primary catalyst for the continuation of the program?

These six components are essential to the conduct and continuation of a successful planned gifts program. Each component is integrated into every activity of the twelve-month program outlined in this book.

The Cycle of Giving

Currently, and in the foreseeable future, there will be an unprecedented transfer of wealth from one family's generation to another. The actual amount is difficult to determine, but many financial professionals contend that it could result in tens of trillions of dollars over the next twenty-year period. In addition, a longitudinal examination of philanthropic giving reveals that more than one-third of all contributions are directed to religious organizations and affiliated causes.

While this environment is not reason enough for a church to consider the employment of a planned gifts program, it does support the idea that, if implemented correctly, a church can realize substantial financial resources. However, the primary motivation for the implementation of a planned gifts program should be centered upon the resolve of significant church needs and the advancement of God's work.

A few additional reasons for considering a planned gifts program include:

- Given these uncertain economic times, planned giving offers an alternative way in which financial support can be provided to a church which does not require immediate "out-of-pocket" monies.

- A planned gifts program will not negatively impact a church's annual stewardship, which generally needs to be sustained or enhanced due to increases in operational overhead.

- Deferred gifts can greatly enhance a church's ability to achieve long-term objectives such as building an endowment.

- This type of giving offers congregations an additional way to demonstrate sacrifice as well as commitment to the will and works of God.

People are often unsure of the definition of "planned giving." A gift is "planned" to the extent that the donor purposefully integrates a charitable gift into the donor's overall financial, tax, and estate planning. A planned gift enables a donor to make a positive financial difference for themselves and for their family, while also providing an important gift to a church. Planned gifts are often thought of as leaving a legacy that benefits not only the donor and the donor's family, but also future generations. Planned giving may take the form of:

- Bequests in a will
- Beneficiary of retirement plan assets
- Beneficiary and/or owner of an existing life insurance policy

In addition, there are other options, which tend to be more complex, including:

- Life income gift
- Charitable remainder trusts
- Charitable lead trusts

For the purpose of this resource guide, specific technical information on the planned giving vehicles is outside the intended scope. In many cases, members of the clergy, administration, or volunteers should seek advice from appropriate counsel, such as attorneys and/or tax advisors.

Instead, this manual offers a detailed implementation model and framework with a primary goal of securing a significant number of planned gifts for a church of any denomination or size. As far as a specific premise, any effort that requires ample human and financial resources should result in an equally significant dividend. In the case of this effort, when employed in the prescribed manner, the return on investment can amount to acquisition of approximately 25 percent or more of worshippers participating in the program.

Thus, the corresponding materials are designed in a manner such that:

- A church can successfully implement a comprehensive and rewarding planned gifts program over a twelve-month period of time.
- A church does not have to engage the services of outside counsel and incur expensive consulting fees.

- The church can utilize a volunteer (worshippers-based and -driven) structure to implement the process.
- The church can implement the process on a step-by-step basis resulting in monthly outcomes and achievements.

Any kind of fundraising program should have a goal of maximizing every potential and desired outcome, including the financial return. In order to accomplish this goal, the strategy needs to be centered around a compelling case that results in significant levels of change; it should be well organized and structured to enhance efficiency and, thus, respectful of volunteer time and resources; and finally, it should offer roles and responsibilities to engage as many individuals in the implementation process as possible to create a sense of ownership and common direction.

Further, while the principles used in this model are geared toward the implementation of a planned gifts program, they can be easily utilized and incorporated into other fundraising activities such as annual drives, targeted gifts (single initiative), and comprehensive major (multi-initiative) and capital (building) gifts campaigns.

The following chapters are designed to accommodate the above processes and products. The model is a building-block tactic that provides all of the tools, attachments, and examples necessary to break down a monumental undertaking into twelve smaller manageable units. As such, each "monthly chapter" contains common resources driven by an agenda, a review of the previous month's activities, a plan of campaign, a communication sequence, and all of the corresponding examples. Examples for each of the chapters is provided electronically.

Maintaining momentum is critical. Therefore, measures should be taken to fully complete each of the stated objectives and activities within each of the twelve chapters (months). If done so, a level of high momentum will be realized and result in significantly larger gifts, the timely enlistment of key and influential volunteers to carry the weight of the campaign, and the full completion (closure) of the campaign.

This manual is organized in twelve monthly subsets. Each subset is interrelated and used in a "building-block" approach. It is designed to be a self-directed, self-contained implementation model and inclusive of all necessary support materials. The employed strategy is grounded in widely accepted fundraising principles and methodologies. We will look at each component in detail (as stated in each month's objectives at the beginning of each chapter) as we move through the program.

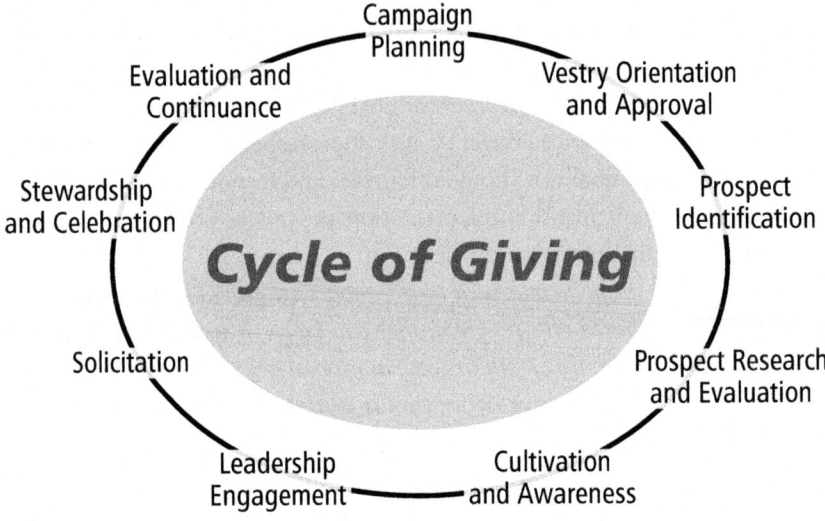

Master Documents

Master Schedule

Task	1	2	3	4	5	6	7	8	9	10	11	12
Planning, Research, and Cultivation												
Confirm intent to employ program.	▓	▓	▓									
Identify and enlist campaign leadership.	▓	▓	▓									
Review/modify gift policies and procedures.	▓	▓	▓									
Review, adjust, and finalize "Master Schedule."	▓	▓										
Complete "Case for Support."		▓	▓									
Complete campaign support materials.			▓	▓								
Identify and assign prospects.			▓	▓								
Construct Organization Chart.			▓									
Develop solicitation materials.			▓	▓								
Cultivation and Solicitation												
Complete church orientation.				▓								
Implement "Communications Sequence."				▓	▓	▓	▓	▓	▓	▓	▓	
Solicit Church Board and volunteers.				▓	▓							
Conduct volunteer training.					▓							
Solicit active parishioners.					▓	▓	▓					
Solicit remaining prospect groups.							▓	▓	▓			
Finalize recognition.										▓	▓	
Evaluation and Continuance												
Hold Taskforce meetings.		▓		▓		▓		▓		▓		
Provide update to Church Board.			▓			▓			▓			▓
Finalize "Plan of Campaign."			▓									
Develop campaign reporting.			▓	▓								
Begin stewardship.											▓	▓
Implement follow-up activities.										▓	▓	▓
Victory Celebration												
Hold victory celebration.											▓	

Plan of Campaign

The "Plan of Campaign" is used as a measure of accountability and tracking for the planned giving campaign. As such, it is utilized beginning in Month 3 when the majority of volunteers have been enlisted. Each month, the "Plan of Campaign" is reviewed by the Planned Gifts Taskforce to determine the extent and status of the activities and tasks completed in addition to planning for upcoming activities and tasks. The "Plan of Campaign" can also be used to assist in enlisting key volunteers.

The goal of the planned giving campaign is to plan and implement activities that will increase the endowment for the [CHURCH]. The goal will be achieved through implementation of the following objectives:

- Development of a plan of action (planned gifts campaign)
- Participation in effective training
- Establishment of a Planned Gifts Taskforce
- Development of appropriate support materials
- Identification of prospective donors
- Determination of cultivation techniques
- Implementation of the program and conduct of solicitations
- Provision of appropriate recognition and stewardship
- Evaluation of campaign status

Month 3—Planning

- Complete enlistment of key volunteers to serve on the Taskforce (minimum of twelve, plus co-chairs).
- Hold the first Taskforce meeting and schedule the dates, times, and locations for the remaining eight monthly planning meetings.

- Provide an initial orientation to the Taskforce members on the "Organizational Structure," "Plan of Campaign," volunteer duties, and timeframes of the campaign.
- Confirm program's intent and use of acquired funds.
- Assign primary responsibility for the "Case for Support" to a member of the Taskforce.
- Confirm the broad-based initiatives that will be included in the "Case for Support" as outlined in the "Strategic Needs Listing" (Exhibit 2-5), including the broad-based areas for support and the associated costs.
- Assign primary responsibility of the "Communications Sequence" to a member of the Taskforce.
- Discuss and recommend specific strategies for awareness/promotion and recognition.
- Begin the "Communications Sequence," which will include a formalized resolution demonstrating support from the Church Board for the planned gifts program.
- Develop and distribute a church notification describing the need for and implementation of the planned gifts program.
- Begin the listing of appropriate prospect and donor base management—identify members of the Church Board, other church groups, former Church Board members, and a complete listing of parishioners.
- Revise the "Plan of Campaign" as needed.

Month 4—Planning, Awareness, and Solicitation

- Hold Taskforce meeting and distribute all necessary materials.
- Continue with "Communications Sequence" activities:
  - Church notification—bulletin, church newsletter, service announcements
  - Preparation for presentation to congregation
  - Continue preparation and finalization of resolution and schedule the reading during the Sunday services (Resolution Sunday).
- Schedule a general meeting for the church that will focus on planned giving.

- Discuss formation of a "planned gifts founders' society."
- Develop outline of "Case for Support" to include logo, theme (if necessary), historical information, initiative detail, and "Ways to Give."
- Begin work on campaign collateral materials such as letterhead (if necessary) and "Letter of Intent."
- Finalize "Plan of Campaign," "Organizational Structure," and "Master Schedule."
- Continue preparation and finalization of necessary policies to support the planned gifts program (if necessary).
- Enlist any additional Taskforce members (if necessary).
- Continue prospect identification (listing of all parishioners).
- Review the duties of the Taskforce members in detail and confirm intent to participate (including providing a planned gift when asked to do so).
- Discuss strategies for solicitation—techniques, timing, and prospects.
- Solicit Taskforce co-chairs and acquire gifts.
- Begin preparation of forms to report progress in terms of number of gifts, types of gifts, and potential revenue (gift report and control sheets).

Month 5—Awareness and Solicitation

- Hold Taskforce meeting and distribute necessary materials.
- Continue with "Communications Sequence":
  – Church notification—bulletin, newsletter, service announcements, etc.
  – Hold church-wide meeting and present planned gifts program—complete presentation on planned giving project and the associated initiatives.
  – Introduce Taskforce membership to congregation.
- Continue discussion of formation of a "planned gifts founders' society."
- Complete solicitation of all Taskforce members.
- Present resolution to parishioners and formal announcement of program goals and opportunities.

- Mail letter announcing planned gifts program to all parishioners.
- Draft narrative for "Case for Support" focusing on the finalization of the historical overview/timeline of the church and drafting of the initiatives.
- Complete draft/layout and design of the "Case for Support," including "Ways to Give," campaign logo, graphics, "Letter of Intent," and proposal letter.
- Provide update to Church Board and discuss importance of 100 percent participation by Church Board membership.
- Prepare a planned giving solicitation proposal draft (letter).
- Determine initial listing of individuals who have existing planned gifts and those who have already expressed an interest in a planned giving arrangement—continue to segment prospect base.
- Confirm and implement strategies for awareness and promotion.
- Confirm enlistment of Taskforce members (if deemed necessary).
- Update and disseminate campaign finance reports to Church Board.
- Schedule Church Board meeting and prepare presentation.

Month 6—Awareness and Solicitation

- Hold Taskforce meeting and distribute necessary materials.
- Complete gift/donor report and submit to Taskforce and Church Board.
- Print all campaign support materials.
- Continue "Communications Sequence."
- Discuss possibility of naming opportunities and plaques.
- Train Taskforce members on solicitation techniques.
- Discuss formation of "founders' society."
- Complete planned giving "Case for Support" and collateral materials—thoroughly edit all materials.
- Confirm segmented list of initial planned giving participants.
- Confirm existing planned giving participants—establish a personal relationship and propose testimonials.

- Prepare an appropriate newsletter article about a planned giving donor—continue with "Communications Sequence."
- Begin to prepare and disseminate monthly newsletters on planned giving (during six-month campaign) and then on quarterly basis.
- Send letter of inquiry for all individuals expressing interest in planned gifts opportunities.
- Announce to congregation (verbally) and through service bulletins, newsletters, and Church newsletter the establishment of "giving society" and "founders' recognition."
- Discuss and schedule appropriate presentations on wills and trusts and financial planning.
- Begin preparation for founders' dinner and celebration.
- Begin discussion on "Wall of Honor" (plaque) for founders.
- Solicit Church Board members for planned gifts.
- Begin scheduling solicitation meetings with initial prospect base (twelve individuals/families)—Group 1.
- Update and disseminate campaign finance reports to Church Board.

Month 7—Awareness and Solicitation

- Hold Taskforce meeting and distribute necessary materials.
- Complete gift/donor report and submit to Taskforce and Church Board.
- Print and acquire "Case for Support" and collateral materials.
- Begin preparation of all solicitation packets and disseminate to volunteers—including proposal letter.
- Continue "Communications Sequence."
- Complete solicitation and acquire 100 percent participation of Taskforce co-chairs, Taskforce members, and Church Board.
- Complete solicitation of Group 1 prospects (twelve individuals).
- Identify Group 2 prospects (twenty-four individuals/families) and begin scheduling solicitation meetings.
- Respond to appropriate inquiries with correspondence and scheduled meetings.

- Hold appropriate cultivation and awareness meetings and individual sessions.
- Send appropriate "thank-you" notes to those individuals participating.
- Continue initial preparation for founders' dinner and celebration.
- Hold appropriate presentations on planned gifts techniques and opportunities.
- Continue discussion on "Wall of Honor" (plaques).
- Continue dissemination of materials, newsletters, and bulletins on planned giving, including testimonials.
- Confirm strategies for recognition, i.e., creation of "society" dinner, lapel pins, etc.
- Update and disseminate campaign finance reports to Church Board.

Month 8—Awareness and Solicitation

- Hold Taskforce meeting and distribute necessary materials.
- Respond to appropriate inquiries with correspondence and scheduled meetings.
- Complete gift/donor report and submit to Taskforce and Church Board.
- Hold appropriate cultivation and awareness meetings and individual sessions.
- Send appropriate "thank-you" notes to those individuals participating.
- Continue preparations for founders' dinner and celebration.
- Hold appropriate presentations on planned gifts techniques and opportunities.
- Continue discussion on "Wall of Honor."
- Continue dissemination of materials, newsletters, and bulletins on planned giving, including testimonials.
- Confirm strategies for recognition, i.e., creation of "society" dinner, lapel pins, etc.
- Update and disseminate campaign finance reports to Church Board.

Month 9—Awareness and Solicitation

- Hold Taskforce meeting and distribute necessary materials.
- Complete gift/donor report and submit to Taskforce and Church Board.
- Provide solicitation status to Church Board on Taskforce, Church Board, Group 1, and Group 2.
- Continue solicitation of segmented prospect base presenting planned gifts proposals and "Case for Support" (Group 2—twenty-four individuals/families).
- Begin discussion of banquet time, place, and preparation.
- Confirm content of initial prospect base solicitations (Group 1).
- Disseminate any necessary solicitation materials to volunteers.
- Identify Group 3 prospects (twenty-four individuals/families) and begin scheduling solicitation meetings.
- Continue preparation for founders' dinner and celebration.
- Hold appropriate presentations on planned gifts techniques and opportunities.
- Hold appropriate cultivation and awareness meetings and individual sessions.
- Respond to appropriate inquiries with correspondences and scheduled meetings.
- Continue preparation for founders' dinner and celebration—and promote.
- Continue development of "Wall of Honor" (plaque).
- Continue dissemination of materials, newsletters, and bulletins, including testimonials.
- Update and disseminate campaign finance reports to Church Board.

Month 10—Awareness and Solicitation

- Hold Taskforce meeting and distribute necessary materials.
- Complete gift/donor report and submit to Taskforce and Church Board.

- Continue "Communications Sequence."
- Provide solicitation status to Church Board on the following:
  - Group 1 (twelve individuals/families)
  - Group 2 (twenty-four individuals/families)
  - Group 3 (twenty-four individuals/families)
  - Group 4 (twenty-four individuals/families)
- Continue solicitation of Group 3 prospects—presenting planned gifts proposal and "Case for Support."
- Confirm content of initial prospect base solicitations (Group 2).
- Identify final grouping of segmented prospect base, Group 4, and begin scheduling solicitation meetings.
- Continue discussion and planning of banquet.
- Initiate naming opportunities and plaque development.
- Confirm content of second segmented prospect base (Group 2).
- Schedule remaining solicitation presentations.
- Hold appropriate presentations on planned gifts techniques and opportunities.
- Hold appropriate cultivation and awareness meetings and individual sessions.
- Respond to appropriate inquiries with correspondence and scheduled meetings.
- Continue preparation for and begin promoting founders' dinner and celebration.
- Continue development of "Wall of Honor" (plaques).
- Continue dissemination of materials, newsletter, and bulletins, including testimonials.
- Update and disseminate campaign finance reports to Church Board.

Month 11—Solicitation

- Hold Taskforce meeting and distribute necessary materials.
- Complete final "Communications Sequence" pieces.

Plan of Campaign

- Review schedule and activity.
- Other strategies
- Complete final preparations for banquet: group: time/place/preparations.
- Provide solicitation status to Church Board on:
  - Group 1 (twelve individuals/families)
  - Group 2 (twenty-four individuals/families)
  - Group 3 (twenty-four individuals/families)
  - Group 4 (twenty-four individuals/families)
- Continue solicitation of Group 3 and Group 4 prospects—presenting planned gifts proposal and "Case for Support."
- Continue solicitation of remaining prospect base—open appeal.
- Finalize intent of segmented prospect base (Group 2).
- Confirm intent of segmented prospect base (Group 3).
- Begin solicitation of Group 4 (twenty-four individuals/families).
- Finalize open appeal (ongoing basis).
- Finalize plans for continuation of planned gifts program and provide orientation to Church Board and Endowment Committee.
- Hold unveiling of "Wall of Honor."
- Disseminate newsletter announcing founding of "society."
- Complete gift/donor report and submit to Church Board.
- Hold banquet debriefing.
- Complete plaque submission requirements.
- Send "society" membership communication and invitation to banquet.
- Complete gift/donor report and provide to Taskforce and Church Board.
- Update and disseminate campaign finance reports to Church Board.

Month 12—Wrap-Up and Celebration

- Hold Taskforce meeting and distribute necessary materials—final meeting.

- Provide solicitation status to Church Board on participation of:
  - Church Board
  - Taskforce members
  - Group 1 (twelve individuals/families)
  - Group 2 (twenty-four individuals/families)
  - Group 3 (twenty-four individuals/families)
  - Group 4 (twenty-four individuals/families)
  - Open appeal
- Acquire 100 percent participation of all four prospect groups (amounting to a minimum of 25 percent of parishioners).
- Complete gift/donor report and provide to Taskforce and Church Board.
- Finalize all details for banquet and hold.
- Acquire plaque.
- Complete last "Communications Sequence"—church-wide campaign status, thank you, and final announcement of banquet.
- Provide stewardship committee with recommendations for follow-up and continuance.
- Update and disseminate campaign finance reports to Church Board.

"Organizational Structure"

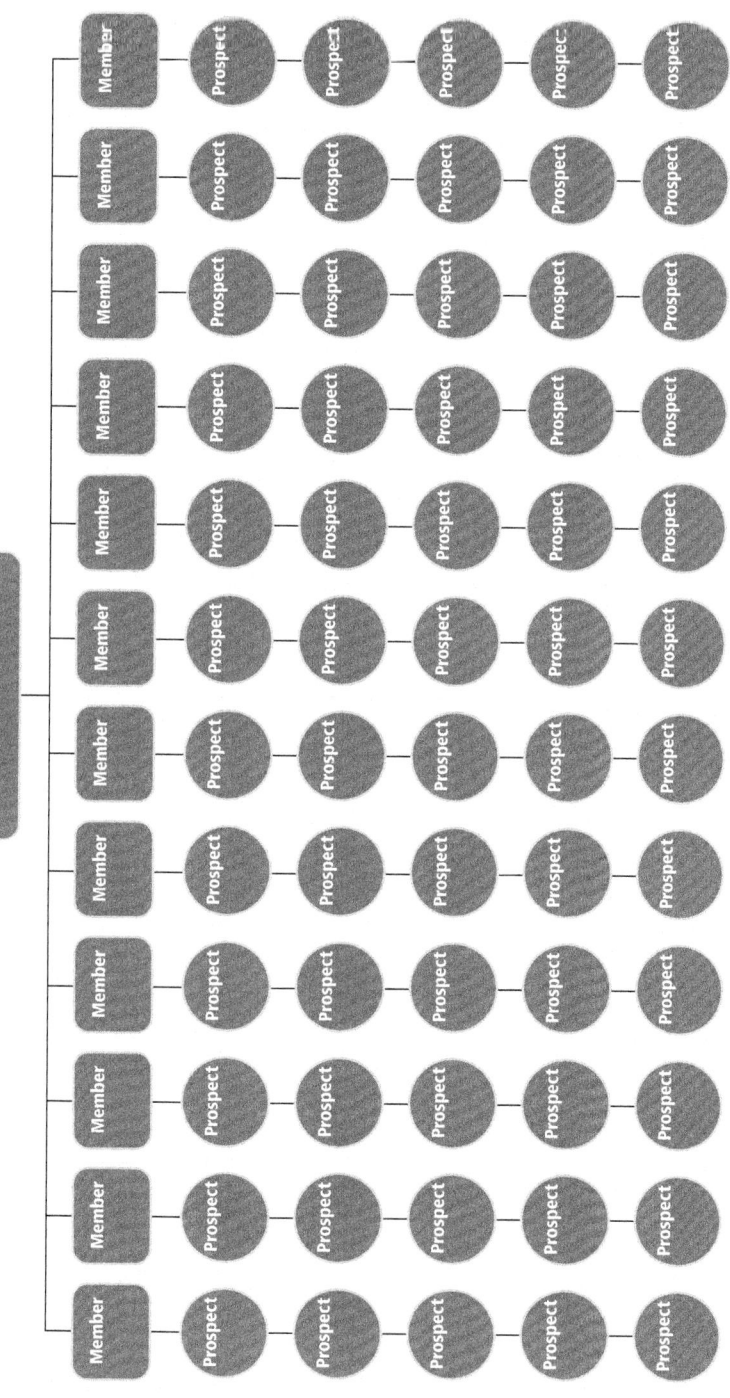

Solicitation Process

The process of solicitation should be formalized as a means of maximizing the outcomes and demonstrating appreciation and respect. The process as outlined below, while it will require some time and planning, is intended to meet the goals of solicitation.

Goals

- Confirm Taskforce member assignments for the prospects in Group 2 in accordance with the grouping strategy.
- Confirm the receipt of "Letter of Intent" from all prospects associated with Group 1.
- Conduct twelve solicitations (Group 1) and realize 100 percent participation.

Process

- During the prospect meeting (Group 2):
  - Review the discussions of the campaign initiatives and the impact that they will have on the church—as embodied in the "Case for Support."
  - Review the status of the campaign—indicating 100 percent of Church Board participation and the results of the Group 1 solicitations.
  - Give your personal views of the campaign and the church.
  - Review "Ways to Give" which will offer different vehicles for participation—and forms of recognition.

- Make the request in the following manner:
  "We hope you will consider participation in the [name of planned gifts program]. Our goal is to extend an invitation to 100 percent of our parishioners. Accomplishment of this goal will be a significant development in our church's ability to advance God's work. Whatever you give after thinking the matter over carefully will be gratefully received and deeply appreciated."
- Suggest that the prospective donor(s) consider the information for a few days before making a pledge.
• During the second Church Board meeting:
  - Provide an update on the campaign proceedings.
  - Disseminate the "Letter of Intent" to all prospects and inform the individual that they should consider the gift with family members, contact the church office or Taskforce members if they have questions, and feel free to drop the "Letter of Intent" to the church office at their convenience or bring it to the next Church Board meeting.
  - Have additional "Letters of Intent" available.
  - Finalize gift decisions.
  - Confirm any additional interest and timing.
  - Have donor(s) complete and sign the "Letter of Intent."
  - Once the "Letter of Intent" has been received, a "thank-you" note should be mailed to the prospect within seventy-two hours. The ideal letter is handwritten and personalized. It should be completed by the clergy or volunteer responsible for the gift receipt.

Outcomes

- Number of volunteers identified—fourteen
- Number of volunteers engaged—fourteen
- Number of volunteers solicited—fourteen
- Total number of volunteer gifts closed—fourteen
  - Two co-chairs
  - Twelve Taskforce members

- Number of prospects identified—seventy-two (twelve Church Board and Group 1–4 prospects)
- Number of prospects cultivated—seventy-two (twelve Church Board and Group 1–4 prospects)
- Number of prospects solicited—thirty-six (twelve Church Board members; twelve Group 1 prospects; and twelve Group 2 prospects)
- Number of total gifts closed:
  - Volunteers—fourteen
  - Church Board—twelve
  - Group 1—twelve
  - Group 2—twelve

Month *by* Month

MONTH 1

Preparation, Prospect Research, and Cultivation

Objectives

- Confirm the intent of the church to move forward with a planned gifts program.
- Set up the management structure, including Taskforce co-chairs and proposed Taskforce members.
- Review planned gift-related policies and procedures.
- Begin discussion of the initiatives to be included in the "Case for Support."
- Determine and confirm specific strategies/timelines as included in the "Master Schedule."

Organizational Meeting

The first steps in implementing your church's planned gifts program is the organization of the management structure to support the program, the creation of planned gifts policies and procedures, the identification of initiatives to be included in the "Case for Support," and the confirmation of timelines. To accomplish these tasks, an initial meeting should be conducted with the following individuals in attendance:

- Clergy
- Church Board chair
- Church Board vice chair

- Stewardship Committee chair
- Church administrator (or an equivalent person)

Prior to the meeting, each individual should be provided with the following items for review:

- Organizational Meeting Agenda: Month 1 (Exhibit 1-1)
- Month 1—Prayer (Exhibit 1-2)
- Month 1: "Tasks to Be Completed" (Exhibit 1-3)
- Qualifications of Taskforce Co-Chairs (Exhibit 1-4)
- Duties of Taskforce Co-Chairs (Exhibit 1-5)
- Planned Gifts Taskforce Membership (Exhibit 1-6)*
- Endowment Subcommittee Bylaws (Exhibit 1-7)*
- Gift Acceptance Policy (Exhibit 1-8)*

Note: The exhibits marked with an asterisk are found exclusively in the downloadable material. To access this material, go to https://www.churchpublishing.org/legacyofalifetime.

Activities to Be Completed during the Organizational Meeting

The following tasks should be completed during the organizational meeting:

- Review what a planned gifts program will entail.
- Discuss the long-term strategic needs of the church and identify areas of need, including outright pledges, endowment-building, and other associated areas of support.
- Review the "Master Schedule" and adjust as necessary.
- Discuss the qualifications of the planned gifts co-chairs, outline the duties they will be asked to perform, and identify three parishioners who could serve in this capacity.
- Discuss enlistment strategies for the proposed Taskforce co-chairs, including who will enlist them and the timing for doing so.
- Begin identifying a minimum of fifteen to eighteen potential Planned Gifts Taskforce members.

- Discuss strategies to obtain full endorsement and participation of the Church Board in the planned gifts program.
- Review and approve the endowment subcommittee bylaws and the planned gifts acceptance policies (note: both of these items should be finalized for Church Board approval at the next meeting).
- Review the task list for Month 1 and determine individual responsibilities and completion dates.
- Review the agenda for Month 2 and determine the date and time for the next meeting.

EXHIBIT 1-1

Organizational Meeting Agenda: Month 1 (One Hour)

- Welcome and prayer (Exhibit 1-2)
- Overview of planned gifts program
- Goals and objectives
- Review Month 1: "Tasks to Be Completed" (Exhibit 1-3).
- Discuss strategic needs to be resolved by planned gifts program (strategic needs analysis).
- Identify planned gifts program leadership.
- Identify three prospective co-chairs and prioritize.
- Review Taskforce co-chair qualifications (Exhibit 1-4).
- Review Taskforce co-chair duties (Exhibit 1-5).
- List possible names of co-chairs (Exhibit 1-6).*
- Confirm enlistment team.
- Review enlistment materials and edit accordingly.
- Schedule date for completion.
- Review and modify planned gifts policies and procedures (Exhibits 1-7 and 1-8).*
- Review planned gifts policies and procedures.
- Schedule approval from Church Board (if deemed necessary)
- Review Month 1: "Tasks to Be Completed" (Exhibit 1-3).
- Schedule next meeting.
- Adjournment

EXHIBIT 1-2
Month 1—Prayer

Gracious God, we thank you for the abundant blessings you have bestowed on this church since our inception. We pray that we may use our many blessings to do the work of your kingdom in this place.

Help us as we approach this challenge of confirming the intent to move forward with a planned gifts program; open our minds and hearts as we deal with the various details of structure, policies and procedures, strategic needs, leaders, and the tasks to be completed.

Help us to respond to the challenge before us, that our church may move forward in our mission to make disciples for Jesus Christ, to baptize, to teach the faith, and to reach out to those less fortunate in God's creation. Give us hope, courage, and wisdom that we do your will, for our church and for future generations.

With confidence, we ask these things through our Lord and Savior Jesus Christ,

Amen

EXHIBIT 1-3
Month 1: "Tasks to Be Completed"

Task	Person(s)	Due Date	Status (Pending, Completed)
Identify "Case" initiatives.			
Adjust and confirm "Master Schedule."			
Identify and enlist co-chairs.			
Identify potential Taskforce members.			
Orient Church Board to planned gifts program.			
Approve gift acceptance policy (Church Board).			
Confirm date, time, and location for Month 2 meeting.			
Prepare Month 2 meeting materials.			
Other:			

*Other activities will be added to this list as opportunities are identified.

EXHIBIT 1-4
Qualifications of Taskforce Co-Chairs

The motivating force behind any successful appeal is quality leadership. The co-chairs for your planned gifts campaign must be the most influential and vigorous members of your church.

Specifically, these individuals must:

1. Be a person of the highest stature who is recognized as a significant leader capable of influencing others of stature within the church family.
2. Possess the ability to:
   - Serve as the chief executive officer of the planned gifts campaign.
   - Actively lead and inspire all those under him/her.
   - Stimulate the involvement and gifts of all Taskforce members.
3. Be capable of influencing others, willing to enlist others to serve in leadership positions, and ready to solicit others to give to the campaign.
4. Be committed to following the "Plan of Campaign" and suggested schedule.
5. Be persistent and methodical, with an enthusiastic and energetic approach to problem solving.
6. Be accessible and available for meetings during a consecutive eleven-month period of time.

EXHIBIT 1-5
Duties of Taskforce Co-Chairs

The duties of the Planned Gifts Taskforce co-chairs will require eighteen to twenty-four hours of involvement over the course of eleven months. These duties include:

1. Acting as the figurehead of the planned gifts campaign
2. Providing guidance and direction to the campaign management and volunteer base
3. Making his/her own pace-setting pledge when asked to do so
4. Attending all Taskforce meetings
5. Attending the campaign kick-off and offering support and endorsement
6. Participating in public relations activities associated with the campaign
7. Providing assistance with the identification of potential donors and volunteers
8. Providing testimonials of support and commitment to the campaign via the "Communications Sequence"
9. Attending and presenting at the campaign celebration representing the church and offering congratulatory remarks to volunteers and donors

MONTH 2
Planning and Prospect Research

Objectives

- Provide an initial orientation to the Taskforce co-chairs on the "Organizational Structure," "Plan of Campaign," and campaign timeframes.
- Confirm the interest, support, and endorsement of the Church Board.
- Finalize and adopt the planned gifts related policies and guidelines and the subcommittee bylaws.
- Identify and prepare for the enlistment of Taskforce volunteers.
- Discern the strategic needs of the church.

Participants

The activities to be accomplished this month include the orientation of the Planned Gifts Taskforce co-chairs, the identification of fifteen to eighteen potential Taskforce members, the finalization of the planned gifts acceptance policies and the endowment subcommittee bylaws, and the identification of initiatives to be included in the "Case for Support." The following individuals will participate in accomplishing the Month 2 activities:

- Clergy
- Church Board chair
- Church Board vice chair
- Stewardship Committee chair

- Church administrator (or an equivalent person)
- Planned Gifts Taskforce co-chairs

Pre-Meeting Activities to Be Completed

Prior to the meeting, the following tasks should be completed:

- Conduct a needs assessment that identifies, prioritizes, and quantifies the church's needs over a five-year period.
- Finalize the "Master Schedule."
- Enlist the Taskforce co-chairs.
- Orient the Church Board to the planned gifts program.
- Review the endowment subcommittee bylaws and the gifts acceptance policies with the Church Board and make the necessary adjustments.
- Confirm the date, time, location, and attendance for the Month 2 Taskforce meeting.
- Review and update the Month 1: "Tasks to Be Completed."
- Finalize all Month 2 meeting materials.

Meeting Activities to Be Completed

The following tasks should be completed during the organizational meeting:

- Provide an update on the Church Board meeting outcomes related to support and endorsement of the planned gifts program (clergy, board chair, and vice chair).
- Review the strategic needs listing prepared as a part of the strategic needs analysis and discuss the long-term strategic needs of the church, such as outright pledges and endowment-building along with associated areas of support.
- Review the planned gifts fundamentals and reach consensus on the methods and operational aspects of the planned gifts program.
- Review the "Master Schedule" and adjust as necessary.
    - Adjust specific information on the planning, prospect research, and cultivation activities.
    - Review strategies associated with each month as identified in the "Plan of Campaign," paying particular attention to Month 3 activities.

- Review the "Organizational Structure" chart, identifying the co-chairs, and discuss their specific roles, including the importance of setting an example by making a planned gift to the church.
- Review the Taskforce duties.
- Prioritize and finalize the listing of fifteen to eighteen potential Taskforce members (the goal is to acquire a minimum of twelve parishioners to serve on the Taskforce).
- Review the Taskforce enlistment process and determine enlistment assignments based upon relationships and associations.
- Review the Month 2 task list and determine individual responsibilities and completion dates.
- Determine the date, time, and location for the Month 3 meeting.

Exhibits

- Organizational Meeting Agenda: Month 2 (Exhibit 2-1)
- Month 2—Prayer (Exhibit 2-2)
- Month 1: "Tasks Completed" (Exhibit 2-3)
- Church Strategic Needs Analysis (Exhibit 2-4)
- Strategic Needs Listing (Exhibit 2-5)*
- Planned Giving Fundamentals (Exhibit 2-6)
- Taskforce Duties (Exhibit 2-7)
- Taskforce Membership Listing (Exhibit 2-8)*
- Taskforce Enlistment Process (Exhibit 2-9)
- Month 2: "Tasks to Be Completed" (Exhibit 2-10)

EXHIBIT 2-1

Organizational Meeting Agenda: Month 2 (One Hour)

- Welcome and prayer (Exhibit 2-2)
- Review Month 1: "Tasks Completed" (Exhibit 2-3).
- Discuss the church's long-term strategic needs (Exhibits 2-4 and 2-5).*
- Review planned giving fundamentals (Exhibit 2-6).
- Review the "Master Schedule" (page 3) and "Plan of Campaign" (page 5) and adjust as necessary.
- Discuss the "Organizational Structure" (page 15) and the duties of the co-chairs.
- Discuss Taskforce membership.
- Review Taskforce duties (Exhibit 2-7).
- Prioritize listing of twelve to fifteen potential Taskforce members (Exhibit 2-8).*
- Review the Taskforce Enlistment Process (Exhibit 2-9) and determine enlistment assignments.
- Review Month 2: "Tasks to Be Completed" (Exhibit 2-10).
- Schedule next meeting.
- Adjournment

EXHIBIT 2-2

Month 2—Prayer

Prayer of Self-Dedication

Almighty and eternal God, so draw our hearts to you, so guide our minds, so fill our imaginations, so control our wills, that we may be wholly yours, utterly dedicated to you; and then use us, we pray, as you will, and always to your glory and the welfare of your people; through our Lord and Savior Jesus Christ.

Amen

(Book of Common Prayer [BCP], page 832)

EXHIBIT 2-3
Month 1: "Tasks Completed"

Task	Person(s)	Due Date	Status (Pending, Completed)
Identify case initiatives.			
Adjust and confirm "Master Schedule."			
Identify and enlist co-chairs.			
Identify potential Taskforce members.			
Orient Church Board to planned gifts program.			
Approve gift acceptance policy (Church Board).			
Confirm date, time, and location for Month 2 meeting.			
Prepare Month 2 meeting materials.			
Other:			

*Other activities will be added to this list as opportunities are identified.

EXHIBIT 2-4
Church Strategic Needs Analysis

Activity

Quantify and prioritize the church's needs over a five-year period to achieve a predetermined level of growth and development.

Purpose

To establish a list of needs to be shared with significant leaders and potential future donors.

Suggested Procedures (Completed by the Clergy Prior to Month 2 Meeting)

Conduct a needs assessment that identifies, prioritizes, and quantifies the church's needs over a five-year period (this should be a byproduct of the church's strategic planning process). The basic steps for implementing the needs assessment are as follows:

Step 1: Analyze the current status of existing programs and facilities.

Step 2: Determine future trends that will cause increases or decreases in funding, support, service, and function.

Step 3: Based on steps 1 and 2, prepare a summary of needs.

Step 4: Prepare a list of recommended projects that will meet the identified needs.

Step 5: Quantify the projects (costs).

Step 6: Place the projects in one of the following categories:

- Youth
- Outreach
- Pastoral care
- Facilities
- Worship, music, and liturgy
- Christian education

- Senior services
- Christian life activities
- Endowment
- Other

Step 7: Finalize the list of projects by acquiring Church Board input.

EXHIBIT 2-6
Planned Giving Fundamentals

Requirements for Implementation

The plan of implementation will be built upon the following requirements for successful planned giving:

1. A worthy, highly regarded and service-oriented church
2. Clergy commitment
3. A realistic budget
4. A committed, trained, and influential Taskforce
5. A prospect research and tracking system
6. A realistic plan of action (campaign)
7. Sound management that is volunteer-based and driven
8. Patience

Method of Implementation

The selective method of cultivation will be used. Experience has proven this method establishes the highest standards of giving and produces by far the best results in relation to cost. The appeal, therefore, will be made primarily to selected prospective donors evaluated on the basis of their influence, relationship with the church, and accessibility.

The full development of the master prospect list and its evaluation are essential factors in a gift-planning program. This list will be upgraded constantly as new prospects are identified. Success in the gift-planning program lies in the effectiveness with which *the right person can be enlisted to cultivate and solicit each prospect.*

Implementation Steps

1. Volunteer Training

A successful gift-planning program requires a trained taskforce. Before a gift-planning program can be implemented, the volunteer base must be in place. If the church has limited volunteer support, then a decision must be made as to how much time will be committed to gift planning—impacting timelines and "Tasks to Be Completed." A limited commitment to gift planning will generally affect the numbers of gifts as well as the types of gifts that the church receives.

2. Church

Selected volunteers will be organized into the gift-planning taskforce to implement identification, evaluation, cultivation, participation, and solicitation processes.

3. Identification

It will be necessary to identify a list of prospects from which to select those who will ultimately be invited to participate (volunteer) in the program. This list should include all members of the church.

4. Evaluation

A comprehensive research model will be applied to the lists of prospects previously identified. Prospective donors will be segmented on the basis of their relationship with the church, financial ability, and accessibility. Primary consideration will be given to major outright gifts.

5. Cultivation

Cultivation involves a variety of awareness activities that will introduce individuals to the church's "Case for Support" and to its vision, mission, and areas of growth.

6. Participation

The success of any fundraising program is directly dependent on the enlistment of a cadre of leaders and workers adequate in number to generate a continuous flow of planned gifts prospects. Interest grows when people become involved as active participants in a project; it follows that they are more inclined to make their own contributions and that those contributions will be larger.

7. Solicitation

The selective method of solicitation will be used. Experience has proven this method establishes the highest standards of giving and produces the best results in relation to cost. The appeal will be made to selected prospective donors recommended by the volunteer base.

8. Measuring Progress

While there are usually current gifts of significance during the establishment of the program, realistic and measurable annual goals should be based on the following criteria:

- Number of volunteers identified, engaged, and solicited
- Number of volunteer gifts closed
- Number of prospects identified, cultivated, and solicited
- Number of prospect gifts closed

EXHIBIT 2-7
Taskforce Duties

The duties of the Planned Gifts Taskforce members will require fifteen to eighteen hours of involvement over the course of the campaign. These duties include:

1. Attending monthly Taskforce meetings (ten total)
2. Assisting in the identification, selection, and enlistment of additional Taskforce members (if deemed necessary)
3. Assisting in the identification of prospects capable of providing planned gifts and suggesting potential solicitor(s) for these prospects
4. Assisting in the solicitation of three to four planned gifts as requested by the Taskforce co-chairs
5. Assisting in the selection and enlistment of other campaign leaders as requested by the Taskforce co-chairs
6. Providing specific expertise to advance the process, including publications, case development, and communications
7. Attending awareness, cultivation, celebration, and other events

EXHIBIT 2-9
Taskforce Enlistment Process

1. Select the prospects you will enlist. Make sure that those that you select are individuals that you know on a personal level.
2. Contact your prospects within three days and set up appointments.
3. Each meeting should take about thirty minutes, during which you will:
   - Discuss the initiative and rationale for the planned gifts program.
   - Define what "planned gifts" means (deferred giving).
   - Review the "Master Schedule."
   - Detail the duties of Taskforce members.
   - Provide information on the "Organizational Structure."
   - Review the listing of proposed volunteers.
   - Discuss your personal feelings about the campaign.
   - Issue the call to serve.
4. If they accept, thank them and advise them of the date, time, and location of the next Taskforce meeting.
5. If they do not accept, determine if they are supportive of the church and the campaign and if they are willing to participate when solicited at a later date.
6. Inform the church office and Taskforce co-chairs of the outcome.
7. If you need additional prospects, please contact campaign headquarters.
8. Remember, your best persuasive tools are your own sincerity, interest, and enthusiasm. That is why you have been asked to represent [CHURCH].

EXHIBIT 2-10
Month 2: "Tasks to Be Completed"

Task	Person(s)	Due Date	Status (Pending, Completed)
Finalize the specific church needs and prepare presentation for Month 3 Taskforce meeting.			
Finalize all Month 3 materials.			
Finalize and distribute all enlistment materials, including "Master Schedule," "Organizational Structure," duties, and Taskforce listing.			
Enlist Taskforce members.			
Provide weekly updates to the church office regarding enlistments.			
Update the Organization Chart to reflect enlisted Taskforce members.			
Confirm date, time, and location for Month 3 meeting.			
Prepare Month 3 meeting materials.			
Other:			

*Other activities will be added to this list as opportunities are identified.

MONTH 3

Preparation, Prospect Research, and Cultivation

Objectives

- Provide an initial orientation to the Taskforce members on the "Organizational Structure," "Plan of Campaign," duties, and timeframes of the campaign.
- Begin the development of the "Case for Support," including the listing of strategic needs.
- Initiate prospect research activities.
- Implement the "Communications Sequence."

Participants

The activities to be accomplished this month include the orientation of Planned Gifts Taskforce members to all aspects of the campaign, development of the "Case for Support" narrative and other collateral materials, initiation of prospect research activities, and development and implementation of the awareness and cultivation program through the "Communications Sequence." The following individuals will participate in accomplishing the Month 3 activities:

- Clergy
- Church Board chair and/or vice chair
- Stewardship Committee chair

- Church administrator (or appointee)
- Planned Gifts Taskforce co-chairs (two)
- Planned Gifts Taskforce members (twelve)

Pre-Meeting Activities to Be Completed

Prior to the meeting, the following tasks should be completed:

- Finalize the listing of church needs to be presented to the Taskforce during the Month 3 meeting.

  Note: The needs should be consistent with church priorities and should be general in scope.

- Complete the enlistment of twelve Taskforce members.
- Finalize all necessary Taskforce orientation materials.
- Update the "Organizational Structure" chart, listing all enlisted members of the Taskforce.
- Confirm the date, time, location, and attendance for the Month 3 Taskforce meeting.
- Review and update the Month 2: "Tasks to Be Completed."
- Finalize all Month 3 meeting materials.

Meeting Activities to Be Completed

The following tasks should be completed during the Taskforce meeting:

- Orient Taskforce members to the planned gifts program:
  - Goals and objectives of the program
  - Gift planning fundamentals
  - Duties and expectations
  - "Organizational Structure"
  - Campaign timeline
  - "Plan of Campaign"
  - Prospect identification
  - Campaign support materials

Preparation, Prospect Research, and Cultivation

- Discuss the previously identified long-term strategic needs of the church and assign a Taskforce member to develop the narrative for the "Case for Support."
- Identify and determine timelines for all tasks associated to the development of the "Case for Support," including content approval, proofing, and printing.
- Discuss awareness and cultivation strategies, including the governing board and other leadership group endorsements, identification of individuals associated with the campaign, and presentations during services.
- Identify a Taskforce member to coordinate the "Communications Sequence" and draft Communications 1, 2, and 3.
- Prepare a list of appropriate prospects, including members of the Church Board, members of other church groups, former Church Board members, and parishioners.
- Review and adjust the "Master Schedule" and "Plan of Campaign" (as necessary).
- Review the Month 3 task list and determine individual responsibilities and completion dates.
- Determine the date, time, and location for the Month 4 meeting.

Exhibits

- Organizational Meeting Agenda: Month 3 (Exhibit 3-1)
- Month 3—Prayer (Exhibit 3-2)
- Month 2: "Tasks Completed" (Exhibit 3-3)
- Planned Giving Fundamentals (Exhibit 3-4)*
- Taskforce Duties (Exhibit 3-5)*
- Taskforce Purpose, Membership, and Meeting Schedule (Exhibit 3-6)*
- Church Strategic Needs Analysis (Exhibit 3-7)*
- "Case for Support" Narrative Outline (Exhibit 3-8)
- "Ways to Give" (Exhibit 3-9)
- "Letter of Intent" (Exhibit 3-10)*

- "Communications Sequence" (Exhibit 3-11)
- Communication 1—Resolution—Draft (Exhibit 3-12)*
- Communication 2—Announcement of Planned Gifts Program to All Parishioners (Clergy Letter)—Draft (Exhibit 3-13)*
- Communication 3—Announcement of Planned Gifts Program to All Parishioners (Bulletin)—Draft (Exhibit 3-14)*
- "Prospect Control Sheet" (Exhibit 3-15)*
- Month 3: "Tasks to Be Completed" (Exhibit 3-16)

EXHIBIT 3-1
Organizational Meeting Agenda: Month 3 (One Hour)

1. Welcome and prayer (Exhibit 3-2)
2. Review Month 2: "Tasks Completed" (Exhibit 3-3).
3. Provide an overview of the planned gifts program:
   - Goals and objectives of the program
   - Planned Giving Fundamentals (Exhibit 3-4)*
   - "Master Schedule" (page 3)
   - "Plan of Campaign" (page 5)
   - Planned gifts campaign leadership
   - "Organizational Structure" (page 15)
   - Taskforce Duties (Exhibit 3-5)*
   - Taskforce Purpose, Membership, and Meeting Schedule (Exhibit 3-6)*
4. Discuss the "Case for Support" and Collateral Materials:
   - Church Strategic Needs (Exhibit 3-7)*
   - "Case for Support" Narrative Outline (Exhibit 3-8)
   - "Ways to Give" (Exhibit 3-9)
   - "Letter of Intent" (Exhibit 3-10)*
5. Review the "Communications Sequence" (Exhibit 3-11) and discuss Communication 1 (Exhibit 3-12),* Communication 2 (Exhibit 3-13),* and Communication 3 (Exhibit 3-14).*
6. Discuss compilation of the prospect list and use of the "Control Sheet" (Exhibit 3-15).*
7. Review Month 3: "Tasks to be Completed" (Exhibit 3-16).
8. Schedule next meeting.
9. Adjournment

EXHIBIT 3-2

Month 3—Prayer

Prayer for Wise Use of Talents

Almighty God, you have blessed each of us with unique gifts, and have called us into specific occupations, relationships, and activities using those gifts. Enable us to use our talents to witness to our faith in you and to communicate your love to the people we meet each day. Empower us to be ministers of reconciliation, love, hope, and justice. Keep us steadfast in our commitment to serve actively in your name through Jesus Christ our Lord, Amen

(Occasional Services [Augsburg, 1982], page 148)

EXHIBIT 3-3
Month 2: "Tasks Completed"

Task	Person(s)	Due Date	Status (Pending, Completed)
Finalize the specific church needs and prepare presentation for Month 3 Taskforce meeting.			
Finalize all Month 3 materials.			
Finalize and distribute all enlistment materials, including "Master Schedule," "Organizational Structure," duties, and Taskforce listing.			
Enlist Taskforce members.			
Provide weekly updates to the church office regarding enlistments.			
Update the Organization Chart to reflect enlisted Taskforce members.			
Confirm date, time, and location for Month 3 meeting.			
Prepare Month 3 meeting materials.			
Other:			

*Other activities will be added to this list as opportunities are identified.

EXHIBIT 3-8
"Case for Support" Narrative Outline

1. The message from the clergy:
   - Spiritual vision and inspiration
   - Spiritual change, direction, rationale
   - Spiritual outcomes to be realized
2. The church description
   - History
   - Today
     – Spiritual strengths
     – Spiritual values
   - Tomorrow
3. Visioning process description (how the needed change was discerned)
4. Challenges/Opportunities
   - The way our church is changing
   - Funding reality
   - Projects
     – Church/Community/Spiritual needs
     – Campaign solution
     – Church/Community/Spiritual benefits
5. The message from the co-chairs—call to action

   Note: Fundamental to the "Case for Support" is testimonials from leaders of influence and/or affluence to support projects and campaign process.

EXHIBIT 3-9
"Ways to Give"

Gift of Current Assets or Appreciated Securities

A gift by check may be made outright or pledged over a period of up to five years to the [CHURCH]'s Endowment Fund. Your gift of appreciated securities (stocks, mutual funds, and bonds) held more than one year is exempt from long-term capital gains taxes and, in most cases, enables you to obtain a charitable income tax deduction equal to the market value of the securities.

A Bequest in a Will

The simple insertion of a clause in your will can assure that a lasting gift will be made to the [CHURCH]'s Endowment Fund. A bequest in a will can take the form of a fixed amount of money, a percentage of an estate or its residual, a specific asset, a trust, or the naming of the church as a contingent beneficiary.

Life Insurance Gift

Since almost everyone has some kind of life insurance, leaving a gift to the [CHURCH]'s Endowment Fund is a simple way for you to make a difference. You may make a gift with very little cost by asking your insurance professional to help you:

1. Change an existing policy to name the [CHURCH]'s Endowment Fund as owner and beneficiary.
2. Purchase a new policy and name the [CHURCH]'s Endowment Fund as owner and beneficiary.
3. Designate the [CHURCH]'s Endowment Fund as a beneficiary for all or a portion of the policy proceeds.

Revocable Living Trust

Many people prefer to use a living trust as an alternative to, or in addition to, their will. A clause similar to a will bequest will implement a charitable gift to the [CHURCH]'s Endowment Fund. A revocable living trust allows a gift of assets to be made now while retaining the right to retrieve those assets later if it becomes necessary.

Life Income Gifts

You can take advantage of a gift vehicle known as a charitable remainder trust to provide income for yourself and your spouse for life, and still make a major gift to the [CHURCH]'s Endowment Fund. These trusts, particularly when they are funded with appreciated property, often provide donors increased income as well as favorable tax benefits. For gifts in smaller amounts, a charitable gift annuity or a pooled income fund gift provides similar features and benefits. These three gift vehicles are available through the Church Foundation.

Gifts of IRAs and Other Tax-Deferred Savings

Persons with savings in the form of tax-deferred funds such as Individual Retirement Accounts (IRAs), 401(k) plans, or other qualified retirement plans should seriously consider using these funds for their charitable giving in their estate plans. When individuals are designated as beneficiaries of these funds, they are subject to tax as ordinary income—whereas charitable, tax-exempt organizations are not subject to the income tax and are able to benefit from the full amount. In addition, designating a charity as a beneficiary will take those funds out of one's estate for estate tax purposes. Thus, there can be a significant tax advantage to using these tax-deferred funds for testamentary gifts to charities.

Memorial Gifts

A gift can be made through any of the vehicles discussed above and designated to honor the memory of a loved one. To maintain and track the gift as a separate and distinct fund will require the gift to be a certain minimum size, as determined by the policies of the Endowment Board of Trustees.

Note: This information is offered for general information only. It is important for those who may consider using one of the gift vehicles mentioned above to seek the advice of their legal and financial advisors.

EXHIBIT 3-11
"Communications Sequence"

Communication	Description
Month 4	
1	Resolution—Draft
2	Announcement of Planned Gifts Program to All Parishioners (Clergy Letter)—Draft
3	Announcement of Planned Gifts Program to All Parishioners (Bulletin)—Draft

EXHIBIT 3-16
Month 3: "Tasks to Be Completed"

Task	Person(s)	Due Date	Status (Pending, Completed)
Finalize listing of church needs and identify areas of impact.			
Complete enlistment of Taskforce members.			
Orient Taskforce members to the planned gifts program.			
Assign primary responsibility for "Case for Support" development to a Taskforce member.			
Determine timelines for all tasks associated with the development of the "Case for Support."			
Begin development of "Case for Support" narrative.			
Assign primary responsibility for the "Communications Sequence" to a Taskforce member.			
Finalize listing of prospects, including members of the Church Board, members of other church groups, former Church Board members, and parishioners.			

Task	Person(s)	Due Date	Status (Pending, Completed)
Identify specific strategies for awareness, promotion, and recognition.			
Draft "Ways to Give" and "Letter of Intent."			
Draft Communication 1 (Resolution), Communication 2 (Clergy Letter), and Communication 3 (Bulletin announcement).			
Update "Master Schedule" (as necessary).			
Update "Plan of Campaign" (as necessary).			
Update Organization Chart to reflect enlisted Taskforce members.			
Confirm date, time, and location for Month 4 meeting.			
Prepare Month 4 meeting materials.			
Other:			

*Other activities will be added to this list as opportunities are identified.

MONTH 4
Planning, Prospect Research, and Cultivation

Objectives

- Continue to train and orient the Taskforce membership to the campaign process.
- Make necessary assignments to specific functions, such as the "Case for Support" development and "Communications Sequence" implementation.
- Continue with campaign preparation and integration of accountability vehicles.
- Clarify roles and expectations, including the solicitation of all volunteers.

Participants

The activities to be accomplished this month include the continued training and orientation of Planned Gifts Taskforce members to the campaign process, refinement of the "Case for Support" narrative and other collateral materials, refinement of the master prospect list through identification and research, implementation of the "Communications Sequence," and implementation of campaign accountability and benchmarking processes. The following individuals will participate in accomplishing the Month 4 activities:

- Clergy
- Church Board chair and/or vice chair

- Stewardship Committee chair
- Church administrator (or appointee)
- Planned Gifts Taskforce co-chairs (two)
- Planned Gifts Taskforce members (twelve)

Pre-Meeting Activities to Be Completed

- Continue development of the "Case for Support" narrative and collateral materials.
- Enlist any additional Taskforce members (if necessary).
- Review and adjust the "Plan of Campaign" and "Master Schedule" (as appropriate).
- Update the Organization Chart (as appropriate).
- Refine the prospect list through identification and research, and add each prospect to the "Control Sheet."
- Continue discussions regarding specific strategies for awareness, promotion, and recognition.
- Review and finalize "Ways to Give" and "Letter of Intent."
- Begin the "Communications Sequence," which will include a formalized resolution demonstrating support from the Church Board for the planned gifts program, an announcement of the program in the church bulletin, and a letter of introduction to all parishioners from the clergy (Communications 1, 2, and 3).
- Confirm the date, time, location, and attendance for the Month 4 Taskforce meeting.
- Review and update the Month 3: "Tasks to Be Completed."
- Finalize all Month 4 meeting materials.

Meeting Activities to Be Completed

The following tasks should be completed during the Taskforce meeting:
- Review the status of each task delineated on the Month 3: "Tasks to Be Completed" (items completed, partially completed, or not completed) and update the "Master Schedule" and "Plan of Campaign" accordingly.

- Confirm the Taskforce member responsible for developing the "Case for Support" and discuss the following components:
  - Church history
  - Vision or extent of desired change (in accordance to the strategic plan)
  - Description of initiatives (projects) to be resolved through the program
  - "Ways to Give"
  - Design and graphics

  Note: The case will be used as a cultivation, teaching, and solicitation tool. As such, the piece should be self-contained in terms of narrative. A "story" of what the church has been, is currently, and wants to become should be described. The Case Narrative should not exceed four to six pages and should include graphics/pictures depicting parishioners, budgetary items, and other items necessary to break up the narrative portion.

- Confirm the Taskforce member responsible for implementation of the "Communications Sequence" and discuss the following:
  - Timing of communications
  - Introduction of the Taskforce and presentation of the resolution (Communication 1) during the announcements at the next week's service(s)
  - A letter from the clergy to parishioners announcing the planned gifts program (Communication 2)
  - Announcement of the planned gifts program in a church-wide publication (Communication 3)
  - Discuss the merits of making a church-wide presentation (possibly in Month 6).

Note: It is important to maintain a constant and regular series of communications to the church. The ongoing articles in the church-wide publication will detail progress to date, as well as serve as informational materials on various aspects of planned giving.

- Review the "Control Sheet" (which includes each prospect listed in alphabetical order) and determine which five prospects each taskforce member will solicit.

  Note: The basis for making a decision to participate in the program will depend upon the prospects' commitment to the church, level of spirituality, and relationship to the solicitor.
- Review the "Solicitation Process."
- Review the Month 4 task list and determine individual responsibilities and completion dates.

Exhibits

- Organizational Meeting Agenda: Month 4 (Exhibit 4-1)
- Month 4—Prayer (Exhibit 4-2)
- Month 3: "Tasks Completed" (Exhibit 4-3)
- "Master Schedule" (page 3)
- "Plan of Campaign" (page 5)
- Sample "Case for Support" Narrative (Exhibit 4-4)
- "Letter of Intent" (Exhibit 4-5)*
- "Communications Sequence" (Exhibit 4-6)
- Communication 1—Resolution (Exhibit 4-7)*
- Communication 2—Announcement of Planned Gifts Program to All Parishioners (Clergy Letter) (Exhibit 4-8)*
- Communication 3—Announcement of Planned Gifts Program to All Parishioners (Bulletin) (Exhibit 4-9)*
- "Control Sheet" (Exhibit 4-10)*
- Month 4: "Tasks to Be Completed" (Exhibit 4-11)

EXHIBIT 4-1
Organizational Meeting Agenda: Month 4 (one hour)

- Welcome and prayer (Exhibit 4-2)
- Review campaign progress:
  - Month 3: "Tasks Completed" (Exhibit 4-3)
  - "Master Schedule" (page 3)
  - "Plan of Campaign" (page 5)
- Discuss "Case for Support" and collateral materials:
  - "Case for Support" Narrative (Exhibit 4-4)
  - "Letter of Intent" (Exhibit 4-5).
- Review and discuss "Communications Sequence" (Exhibit 4-6):
  - Communication 1—Resolution (Exhibit 4-7)*
  - Communication 2—Announcement of Planned Gifts Program to All Parishioners (Clergy Letter) (Exhibit 4-8)*
  - Communication 3—Announcement of Planned Gifts Program to All Parishioners (Bulletin) (Exhibit 4-9)*
  - Church presentation
- Review prospect identification and research:
  - "Control Sheet" (Exhibit 4-10)*
  - Organization Chart
  - Prospect selection
- Review the "Solicitation Process" (page 17).
- Review Month 4: "Tasks to Be Completed" (Exhibit 4-11).
- Schedule next meeting.
- Adjournment

EXHIBIT 4-2

Month 4—Prayer

A Prayer for Stewardship of Treasure

Almighty God, whose loving hand has given me all that I possess, grant me the grace to honor you with my substance. Help me to see that I am unworthy of your blessings unless I find some way to share them with others. Bless our efforts as I remember that one day I must give account to you. Grant me the courage and commitment to be faithful in my tithe and offerings, thereby presenting myself to you as a faithful steward of all that you give me through Jesus Christ my Lord and Savior.

Amen

(BCP, page 827)

EXHIBIT 4-3
Month 3: "Tasks Completed"

Task	Status (Partially Completed, Completed, Not Completed)
Finalize listing of church needs and identify areas of impact.	
Complete enlistment of Taskforce members.	
Orient Taskforce members to the planned gifts program.	
Assign primary responsibility for "Case for Support" development to a Taskforce member.	
Determine timelines for all tasks associated with the development of the "Case for Support."	
Begin development of "Case for Support" narrative.	
Assign primary responsibility for the "Communications Sequence" to a Taskforce member.	
Finalize listing of prospects, including members of the Church Board, members of other church groups, former Church Board members, and parishioners.	
Identify specific strategies for awareness, promotion, and recognition.	

(continued on page 66)

Task	Status (Partially Completed, Completed, Not Completed)
Draft "Ways to Give" and "Letter of Intent."	
Draft Communication 1 (Resolution), Communication 2 (Clergy Letter), and Communication 3 (Bulletin announcement).	
Update "Master Schedule" (as necessary).	
Update "Plan of Campaign" (as necessary).	
Update Organization Chart to reflect enlisted Taskforce members.	
Confirm date, time, and location for Month 4 meeting.	
Prepare Month 4 meeting materials.	
Other:	

*Other activities will be added to this list as opportunities are identified.

EXHIBIT 4-4
Sample "Case for Support" Narrative

Introduction

You enjoy an inheritance at [CHURCH]. Generations of worshipers knelt before the same altar and prayed the same prayers you pray. The traditional services mark the structure of life—baptism, confirmation, marriage, and burial—just as it marked the lives for those who worshiped before you. You can continue the legacy. Making provision for your church in your will or estate plan helps you share your worship traditions and ministries with those who will come after you.

What better gift could we give ourselves than to know that we have provided for the orderly disposition of the things we have been given in life? What better way for us to show what has really mattered to us in our life? What better blessing than to know that we leave a legacy for our children—a legacy of love of worship at [CHURCH]?

The Parable of the Sower

Matthew 13:1–9

That same day Jesus went out of the house and sat beside the sea. Such great crowds gathered around him that he got into a boat and sat there, while the whole crowd stood on the beach. And he told them many things in parables, saying: "Listen! A sower went out to sow. And as he sowed, some seeds fell on the path, and the birds came and ate them up. Other seeds fell on rocky ground, where they did not have much soil, and they sprang up quickly, since they had no depth of soil. But when the sun rose, they were scorched; and since they had no root, they withered away. Other seeds fell among thorns, and the thorns grew up and choked them. Other seeds fell on good soil and brought forth grain, some hundredfold, some sixty, some thirty. Let anyone with ears listen!"

What Is Planned Giving?

Planned giving is a form of stewardship that encourages parishioners to find new approaches for managing their resources during their lifetime and for leaving a legacy that will contribute generously through their estate. It is one way for a parishioner's life to count in a way that will live beyond them.

The Ministry of Planned Giving

- Presents a ministry that encourages and assists you to plan responsibly for the disposition of your worldly goods.
- Encourages you to make suitable provisions for your family members while remembering the church as well.
- Invites you to witness to your faith, your love for God and the church in a very special way.
- Strengthens the ministry of the church—the institution or the programs you desire to support—for generations to come.

May I Designate My Planned Gift for a Purpose?

Planned gifts are encouraged to be made without restrictions or designations; however, if you feel strongly about designating, you may designate a portion of your gift to one or more of the following church ministries:

- Youth
- Outreach
- Pastoral care
- Facilities
- Worship, music, and liturgy
- Christian education
- Senior services
- Christian life activities

How Is the [CHURCH] Endowment Fund Managed and Used?

The stewardship of the [CHURCH] Endowment Fund is provided by a Standing Committee appointed by the Church Board. It is composed of five parishioners, plus the clergy and board chair serving as ex-officio (non-voting) members. The Endowment Fund holds and administers permanent funds, established in perpetuity. Support of ministries occurs through annual expenditures of only a portion of the fund's earnings. The amount that is made available is determined each year by the Endowment Board, as a percentage of the fund's value. The endowment policy has been established by the Church Board so earnings will be used to develop and enhance ministries and properties beyond what is possible through annual operating monies.

[CHURCH]'s Endowment Fund can receive gifts at any time for its unrestricted funds. Funds restricted to special purposes can be created through larger gifts. In either case, endowment gifts can be made from current income, from assets, or through a "planned gift."

How Do I Make a Planned Gift to [CHURCH]?

Any member of the church Planned Gifts Taskforce or Endowment Committee can assist you in finding the information and resources you may need to explore the possible advantages of making a planned gift. Most planned gifts offer attractive benefits from a tax standpoint. Some of the most common ways to make planned gifts are listed below.

Gift of Current Assets or Appreciated Securities

A gift by check may be made outright or pledged over a period of up to five years to [CHURCH]'s Endowment Fund. Your gift of appreciated securities (stocks, mutual funds, and bonds) held more than one year is exempt from long-term capital gains taxes and, in most cases, enables you to obtain a charitable income tax deduction equal to the market value of the securities.

A Bequest in a Will

The simple insertion of a clause in your will can assure that a lasting gift will be made to [CHURCH]'s Endowment Fund. A bequest in a will can take the form of a fixed amount of money, a percentage of an estate or its residual, a specific asset, a trust, or the naming of the church as a contingent beneficiary.

Life Insurance Gift

Since almost everyone has some kind of life insurance, leaving a gift to [CHURCH]'s Endowment Fund is a simple way for you to make a difference. You may make a gift with very little cost by asking your insurance professional to help you:

- Change an existing policy to name [CHURCH]'s Endowment Fund as owner and beneficiary.

- Purchase a new policy and name [CHURCH]'s Endowment Fund as owner and beneficiary.
- Designate [CHURCH]'s Endowment Fund as a beneficiary for all or a portion of the policy proceeds.

Revocable Living Trust

Many people prefer to use a living trust as an alternative to, or in addition to, their will. A clause similar to a will bequest will implement a charitable gift to [CHURCH]'s Endowment Fund. A revocable living trust allows a gift of assets to be made now while retaining the right to retrieve those assets later if it becomes necessary.

Life Income Gifts

You can take advantage of a gift vehicle known as a charitable remainder trust to provide income for yourself and your spouse for life, and still make a major gift to [CHURCH]'s Endowment Fund. These trusts, particularly when they are funded with appreciated property, often provide donors increased income as well as favorable tax benefits. For gifts in smaller amounts, a charitable gift annuity or a pooled income fund gift provides similar features and benefits. These three gift vehicles are available through the Church Foundation.

Gifts of IRAs and Other Tax-Deferred Savings

Persons with savings in the form of tax-deferred funds such as Individual Retirement Accounts (IRAs), 401(k) plans, or other qualified retirement plans, should seriously consider using these funds for their charitable giving in their estate plans. When individuals are designated as beneficiaries of these funds, they are subject to tax as ordinary income; whereas charitable, tax-exempt organizations are not subject to the income tax and are able to benefit from the full amount. In addition, designating a charity as a beneficiary will take those funds out of one's estate for estate tax purposes. Thus, there can be a significant tax advantage to using these tax-deferred funds for testamentary gifts to charities.

Memorial Gifts

A gift can be made through any of the vehicles discussed above and designated to honor the memory of a loved one. To maintain and track the gift as a separate and distinct fund will require the gift to be a certain minimum size, as determined by the policies of the Endowment Board of Trustees.

Note: This information is offered for general information only. It is important for those who may consider using one of the gift vehicles mentioned above to seek the advice of their legal and financial advisors.

What Is the "Society of the [CHURCH]"?

The rich history and tradition of [CHURCH] has inspired us to continue to nurture and grow our community of faith for future generations by creating "The Society of [CHURCH]." The Society has been established to honor those who include [CHURCH] in their wills or estate plans through a planned gift.

How Can I Become a Member?

[CHURCH] invites you to become a member of "The Society of [CHURCH]." All that is required is your heartfelt commitment of support and a few moments of your time. A planned gift allows for the donation of an asset at a specific future date in one's will or estate plan. Anyone who names [CHURCH] as beneficiary in his or her will or estate plan (or has already done so) and completes and returns the enclosed enrollment form will become a member of the "Society."

If you already have a will or trust, you need not rewrite it. You can add a provision for the church through a simple codicil or amendment. For more information and assistance, contact your attorney, financial advisor, and/or the stewardship office. We are prepared to make this process simple and straightforward for you.

What Are the Rewards of Joining the Society?

Your deep commitment and strong support of [CHURCH] throughout the years have enabled us to foster an environment where the mission and ministry of our church continue to be lived each and every day.

Today's gifts are important because they enable us to grow in our faith and reach out to others. However, "tomorrow's" gifts are equally important because they allow for the future ministry of our church. Through God's grace and your generosity, [CHURCH] will be in a strong position to bring the message of hope in Jesus Christ to the people of [City] well into the twenty-first century and beyond. When you join "The Society of [CHURCH]," you will help assure that generations of people will receive the gifts of hope, prayer, fellowship, and worship for years to come.

As a member of the "Society," you will receive invitations to regularly scheduled tax and financial planning seminars and special events. Also, once a year you will be invited to meet with the clergy and board chairs to discuss the future of [CHURCH].

EXHIBIT 4-6
"Communications Sequence"

Communication	Description
Month 4	
1	Resolution
2	Announcement of Planned Gifts Program to All Parishioners (Clergy Letter)
3	Announcement of Planned Gifts Program to All Parishioners (Bulletin)

EXHIBIT 4-11
Month 4: "Tasks to Be Completed"

Task	Person(s)	Due Date	Status (Pending, Completed)
Update "Master Schedule" (as necessary).			
Update "Plan of Campaign" (as necessary).			
Update Organization Chart (as necessary).			
Continue development of the "Case for Support" narrative and collateral materials.			
Develop "Communications Sequence," including types of communications and timelines for implementation.			
Finalize Communication 1 (Resolution), Communication 2 (Clergy Letter), and Communication 3 (Bulletin announcement).			
Determine if a church-wide presentation is appropriate (would take place in Month 6).			

Task	Person(s)	Due Date	Status (Pending, Completed)
Update the "Control Sheet" to include solicitation assignments (a total of seventy-four individuals should be identified for solicitation).			
Finalize and print "Ways to Give" and "Letter of Intent."			
Solicit the Taskforce co-chairs (clergy).			
Begin solicitation meetings with twelve Taskforce members (co-chairs).			
Confirm date, time, and location for Month 5 meeting.			
Prepare Month 5 meeting materials.			
Other:			

Other activities will be added to this list as opportunities are identified.

MONTH 5
Planning, Prospect Research, Cultivation, and Solicitation

Objectives

- Continue with campaign accountability and benchmarking processes, including use of the "Tasks to Be Completed," "Master Schedule," and "Plan of Campaign," and evaluate and adjust accordingly.
- Draft all "Case for Support" narrative pieces.
- Delegate and confirm the master prospect list to volunteers.
- Implement the awareness and cultivation program via the "Communications Sequence."
- Acquire gifts from selected volunteers and Church Board.

Participants

The activities to be accomplished this month include the continued development of the "Case for Support" and collateral materials, the delegation of prospects to volunteers, the continued implementation of the "Communications Sequence," and the solicitation of selected volunteers and Church Board. The following individuals will participate in accomplishing the Month 5 activities:

- Clergy
- Church Board chair or vice chair
- Stewardship Committee chair

- Church administrator (or appointee)
- Planned Gifts Taskforce co-chairs (two)
- Planned Gifts Taskforce members (twelve)

Pre-Meeting Activities to Be Completed

- Review and update the "Master Schedule" and control sheets.
- Revise the "Plan of Campaign" (as necessary).
- Update the Organization Chart to include assignments of all volunteer prospect selections.
- Continue the drafting of the "Case for Support" narrative and print "Letter of Intent."
- Discuss and recommend specific strategies for awareness/promotion and recognition to include the clergy awareness sessions and leadership awareness sessions, and prepare the necessary materials.
- Update and revise the "Communications Sequence."
- Confirm the date, time, location, and attendance for the Month 5 Taskforce meeting.
- Review and update the Month 4: "Tasks to Be Completed."
- Finalize all Month 5 meeting materials.

Meeting Activities to Be Completed

The following tasks should be completed during the Taskforce meeting:

- The previous month's "Tasks Completed" should be reviewed and status of each item detailed. Items that have been completed, partially completed, or not completed should be identified on the "Master Schedule" and "Plan of Campaign." Timelines for the latter two categories should be discerned for completion. The names of Taskforce members assigned to the task completion should be identified.
- The Taskforce member responsible for the "Communications Sequence" should be confirmed. The "Communications Sequence" should be reviewed and dates of submissions detailed, including Communications 1, 2, and 3. The final version of Communications 4, 5, and 6 should be drafted and scheduled for dissemination.

Planning, Prospect Research, Cultivation, and Solicitation

- The decision to offer a church-wide presentation should be made. If deemed necessary, the presentation should be reviewed and modified. Information on the campaign initiatives, leadership, and timing should be included in the presentation. Approximately thirty minutes will be required for the presentation. It is recommended that the presentation be scheduled between Sunday services and completed by the co-chairs and/or Taskforce members. Members of the Church Board should be in attendance as a means of demonstrating support and endorsement.
- During the course of the meeting, an update on solicitations to date should occur. Confirmation of the co-chairs (two) and team members (twelve) gifts should be realized with "Letter of Intent" submitted to the church office. A schedule for prospect solicitations can be discussed; however, no solicitations should occur until attainment of the "Case for Support." A presentation to the Church Board should be scheduled for the purpose of campaign update and challenge of 100 percent participation.
- Individuals responsible for the completion of the activities ("Tasks to be Completed") as well as associated dates will be determined.

Post-Meeting Activities to Be Completed

- Update all campaign accountability and benchmark forms ("Master Schedule," "Plan of Campaign," and monthly "Tasks to Be Completed").
- Complete the Case Narrative.
- Communications 4, 5, and 6 should be revised and disseminated according to the schedule.
- The time and location of a church-wide presentation will be determined and confirmed. The presentation should be reviewed and modified with inclusions to the campaign initiatives, leadership, and timing.
- The "Control Sheet" should be updated, which will include assignments of Taskforce co-chairs and members to prospects. A total of seventy-four individuals should be identified for solicitation purposes—two co-chairs (to be conducted by the clergy), twelve

Taskforce members (to be conducted by the co-chairs), and sixty parishioners (to be conducted by the twelve Taskforce members).
- The gifts of the co-chairs of the Taskforce should be received. All remaining Taskforce members should be solicited by co-chairs and "Letter of Intent" received.
- Confirm Month 6 meeting—date, time, place, and attendance.
- Update the Month 5: "Tasks to Be Completed" form.
- Generate all necessary materials for Month 6 meeting.

Exhibits

- Organizational Meeting Agenda: Month 5 (Exhibit 5-1)
- Month 5—Prayer (Exhibit 5-2)
- Month 4: "Tasks Completed" (Exhibit 5:3)
- Case Narrative (Exhibit 5-4)*
- "Letter of Intent" (Exhibit 5-5)*
- "Communications Sequence" (Exhibit 5-6)
- Communication 4—Introduction to Planned Gifts Society (Church Mailing) (Exhibit 5-7)*
- Communication 5—Announcement of Planned Gifts Taskforce (Newsletter) (Exhibit 5-8)*
- Communication 6—Invitation to Join "Founders' Society" (Church Mailing) (Exhibit 5-9)*
- "Control Sheet" (Exhibit 5-10)*
- Month 5: "Tasks to Be Completed" (Exhibit 5-11)

EXHIBIT 5-1
Organizational Meeting Agenda: Month 5 (one hour)

- Welcome and overview
- Prayer (Exhibit 5-2)
- Review campaign progress.
  - Review Month 4: "Tasks Completed" (Exhibit 5-3).
  - "Master Schedule" (page 3)
  - "Plan of Campaign" (page 5)
- Discuss and review "Case for Support" and collateral materials:
  - Case Narrative (Exhibit 5-4)*
  - "Letter of Intent" (Exhibit 5-5)*
- Review "Communications Sequence" (Exhibit 5-6):
  - Communication 4—Introduction to Planned Gifts Society (Church Mailing) (Exhibit 5-7)*
  - Communication 5—Planned Gifts Taskforce (Newsletter) (Exhibit 5-8)*
  - Communication 6—Invitation to Join "Founders' Society" (Church Mailing) (Exhibit 5-9)*
- Discuss prospect identification and research:
  - "Control Sheet" (Exhibit 5-10)*
- Discuss "Solicitation Process" (page 17):
  - Team Member Organization Chart
  - Additional team selection—if deemed necessary
- Review Month 5: "Tasks to Be Completed" (Exhibit 5-11).
- Schedule of next meeting.
- Adjournment

EXHIBIT 5-2
Month 5—Prayer

O merciful Creator, your hand is open wide to satisfy the needs of every living creature: Make us always thankful for your loving providence; and grant that we, remembering the account that we must one day give, may be faithful stewards of your good gifts; through Jesus Christ our Lord, who with you and the Holy Spirit lives and reigns, one God, forever and ever.
    Amen

(BCP, page 259)

EXHIBIT 5-3
Month 4: "Tasks Completed"

Task	Status
Update all campaign accountability and benchmark forms ("Master Schedule," "Plan of Campaign," and "Tasks to Be Completed").	
Draft the Case Narrative to include the church history, initiatives (projects), "Ways to Give," and frequently asked questions. In addition, the "Letter of Intent" should be completed and printed.	
The "Communications Sequence" should be completed, including a confirmation of the necessary articles, letters, and announcements. Specific dates should be included.	
Consideration to a church-wide presentation is finalized. If it is deemed necessary, the presentation should be reviewed, modified, and scheduled during Month 6.	
The "Control Sheet" should be updated, which will include assignments of Taskforce co-chairs and members to prospects. A total of seventy-four individuals should be identified for solicitation purposes—two co-chairs to be conducted by the clergy, twelve Taskforce members to be conducted by the co-chairs, and sixty parishioners to be conducted by the twelve Taskforce members.	

(continued on page 84)

Task	Status
The co-chairs of the Taskforce should be solicited by the clergy. The co-chairs should begin scheduling the solicitation of twelve Taskforce members.	
Confirm Month 5 meeting—date, time, place, and attendance.	
Prepare Month 5 meeting materials.	
Other:	

Other activities will be added to this list as opportunities are identified.

EXHIBIT 5-6
"Communications Sequence"

Communication	Description
Month 5	
4	Introduction to Planned Gifts Society (Church Mailing)
5	Announcement of Planned Gifts Taskforce (Newsletter)
6	Invitation to Join "Founders' Society" (Church Mailing)

EXHIBIT 5-11

Month 5: "Tasks to Be Completed"

Task	Person(s)	Due Date	Status (Pending, Completed)
Update all accountability and benchmarking tools.			
Continue with "Communications Sequence" (items 4, 5, and 6) and distribute accordingly.			
Draft "Case for Support," focusing on the finalization of narrative, and begin layout.			
Discuss printing of "Case for Support" and collateral materials ("Letter of Intent").			
Schedule Church Board meeting and prepare presentation—provide update to Church Board and discuss importance of 100 percent participation by Church Board membership.			
Update and disseminate to Church Board campaign finance reports.			
Confirm strategies for awareness and promotion and implementation, including church-wide presentation.			
Revise the planned giving presentation.			

Task	Person(s)	Due Date	Status (Pending, Completed)
Schedule and confirm time and location of church-wide presentation.			
Confirm prospect listing and assignments (Taskforce members).			
Confirm gift receipts from co-chairs and Taskforce members.			
Confirm and complete Month 6: "Tasks to Be Completed."			
Confirm Month 6 meeting—date, time, place, and attendance.			
Prepare Month 6 meeting materials.			
Other:			

*Other activities will be added to this list as opportunities are identified.

MONTH 6
Planning, Prospect Research, Cultivation, and Solicitation

Objectives

- Continue with campaign accountability and benchmarking processes, including use of the "Tasks to Be Completed," "Master Schedule," and "Plan of Campaign," and evaluate and adjust accordingly.
- Modify and complete all "Case for Support" narrative pieces.
- Delegate and confirm the master prospect list to volunteers—and categorize by affinity.
- Implement the awareness and cultivation program via the "Communications Sequence."
- Present overview of planned giving to parishioners and provide update to the Church Board.
- Acquire gifts from 100 percent of volunteers and Church Board.

Participants

- Clergy
- Church Board chair or vice chair
- Stewardship Committee chair
- Church administrator (or appointee)
- Planned Gifts Taskforce co-chairs (two)
- Planned Gifts Taskforce members (twelve)

Pre-Meeting Activities to Be Completed

- Review and update the "Master Schedule," "Tasks Completed," and control sheets.
- Revise "Plan of Campaign" as deemed necessary.
- Upon completion of enlistments, update Organization Chart to include any additional assignments of all prospect selections by volunteers. Identify volunteers/prospects by progress of enlistment (volunteer), cultivated, solicited, and pledged.
- Acquire "Letter of Intent" from all volunteers.
- Update Church Board on campaign proceedings and introduce the concept of the importance of acquiring 100 percent participation of Church Board in the program.
- Discuss and recommend specific strategies for awareness/promotion and recognition to include the clergy awareness sessions—and prepare necessary materials.
- Continue implementation of the "Communications Sequence," including submission of Communications 4, 5, and 6.
- Confirm Month 6 meeting—date, time, place, and attendance.
- Update status of "Tasks Completed."
- Generate all necessary materials for Month 6 meeting.

Meeting Activities to Be Completed

- The previous month's "Tasks Completed" should be reviewed and status of each item detailed. Items that have been completed, partially completed, or not completed should be identified on the "Master Schedule" and "Plan of Campaign." Timelines for the latter two categories should be discerned for completion. The names of Taskforce members assigned to the task completion should be identified.
- The "Communications Sequence" should be reviewed and dates of submissions detailed and confirmed for Communications 1–6. The draft versions of Communications 7, 8, 9, and 10 should be completed.

- The church-wide presentation should be made. Information on the campaign initiatives, leadership, and timing should be provided and detailed in the presentation. Time should be allocated for answering questions that parishioners may have on specific topics. As a part of the presentation, a testimonial by a member of the congregation as well as a representative of the Church Board should be expressed on the meaningfulness of the church. An effort should be made to take attendance as a means of identifying those parishioners who may have an initial interest in the campaign.
- All prospects will be categorized ("Control Sheet") by a number of affinities, including influence and affluence and relationship to the church—as determined by each of the volunteers (Taskforce members). Each member will be defined by a "Group" (Groups 1–4). The Group 1 prospects will be approached first for the purposes of solicitation.
- During the course of the meeting, an update on solicitations to date should occur, including receipt of "Letter of Intent" and expressions of interest. Confirmation of the Taskforce members' (twelve) gifts should be realized with "Letter of Intent" submitted to the church office. All Taskforce member gift accounts should be determined at this juncture. Ideally, a minimum of fourteen gifts should be realized by this point. A schedule for prospect solicitations can be initiated by all Taskforce members; however, no solicitations should occur until attainment of the "Case for Support."
- A presentation to the Church Board should be scheduled and conducted. The goal of 100 percent of Church Board support and participation should be delivered. In addition, a formal endorsement of the program from the Church Board should be obtained. The intent of Church Board members should be ascertained. "Letter of Intent" should be disseminated to all Church Board members.
- The Organization Charts for each of the Taskforce members should be updated. Each of the "cells" for volunteers should contain three letters in each corner ("C-Cultivated; S-Solicited; P-Pledged"). This approach will show progress for gift realization. As each prospect (which is assigned to a Taskforce member) is cultivated, then the corresponding

letter is circled. The same holds true for "soliciting" and "pledged" (when a "Letter of Intent" is received).

- Specific tasks will be delineated using Exhibit 6-11. Individuals responsible for the completion of the activities as well as associated dates will be determined.

Post-Meeting Activities to Be Completed

1. Update all campaign accountability and benchmark forms ("Master Schedule," "Plan of Campaign," and "Tasks to Be Completed").
2. Acquire and distribute the printed "Case for Support."
3. Communications 7, 8, 9, and 10 should be revised and disseminated according to the schedule.
4. Determine and confirm the time and location of a church-wide presentation, which should be reviewed and modified with inclusions to the campaign initiatives, leadership, and timing.
5. Update the "Control Sheet," which will include assignments of Taskforce co-chairs and members to prospects. A total of seventy-four individuals should be identified for solicitation purposes.
6. The gifts of the Taskforce members should be received—100 percent.
7. Confirm the Church Board endorsement as well as their intent to participate in the program. Distribute "Letter of Intent" and confirm deadline for solicitation.
8. Initiate scheduling of Taskforce member-prospect solicitations.
9. Confirm Month 7 meeting—date, time, place, and attendance.
10. Update the "Tasks to Be Completed" form.
11. Generate all necessary materials for Month 7 meeting.

Exhibits

- Organizational Meeting Agenda: Month 6 (Exhibit 6-1)
- Month 6—Prayer (Exhibit 6-2)
- Month 5: "Tasks Completed" (Exhibit 6-3)
- "Case for Support" Evaluation (Exhibit 6-4)*

- "Communications Sequence" (Exhibit 6-5)
- Communication 7—Invitation to Church Board to Participate in Planned Gifts Program (Letter from Co-Chairs) (Exhibit 6-6)*
- Communication 8—Invitation to Former Church Board to Participate in Planned Gifts Program (Letter from Co-Chairs) (Exhibit 6-7)*
- Communication 9—Invitation to Taskforce to Participate in Planned Gifts Program (Letter from Co-Chairs) (Exhibit 6-8)*
- Communication 10—Planned Giving Introduction (Bulletin) (Exhibit 6-9)*
- "Control Sheet" (Exhibit 6-10)*
- Month 6: "Tasks to Be Completed" (Exhibit 6-11)

EXHIBIT 6-1
Organizational Meeting Agenda: Month 6 (one hour)

- Welcome and overview
- Prayer (Exhibit 6-2)
- Campaign progress:
  - Review Month 5: "Tasks Completed" (Exhibit 6-3).
  - "Master Schedule" (page 3)
  - "Plan of Campaign" (page 5)
- "Case for Support" Evaluation (Exhibit 6-4)*
- "Communications Sequence" (Exhibit 6-5):
  - Communication 7—Invitation to Church Board—to Participate in Planned Gifts Program (Letter from Co-Chairs) (Exhibit 6-6)*
  - Communication 8—Invitation to Former Church Board to Participate in Planned Gifts Program (Letter from Co-Chairs)(Exhibit 6-7)*
  - Communication 9—Invitation to Taskforce to Participate in Planned Gifts Program (Letter from Co-Chairs) (Exhibit 6-8)*
  - Communication 10—Planned Giving Introduction (Bulletin) (Exhibit 6-9)*
- Prospect identification and research:
  - "Control Sheet" (Exhibit 6-10)*
- "Solicitation Process" (page 17):
  - Organization Chart:
    - Taskforce finalization
    - Church Board intent
    - Group 1 conducts solicitation
- Review Month 6: "Tasks to Be Completed" (Exhibit 6-11).
- Schedule next meeting.
- Adjournment

EXHIBIT 6-2
Month 6—Prayer

O Lord, your Son has taught us that from those to whom much is given, much will be required. Guide us to obtain our monetary resources honestly, neither injuring our neighbors nor ravaging your creation. And help us to use wisely what has been entrusted to us, for the well-being of our families and all people, and for the strengthening of your kingdom in justice, beauty, peace, and parochial ministries through Jesus Christ our Lord.
   Amen

(Adapted Prayers and Thanksgiving, 1973, page 93)

EXHIBIT 6-3

Month 5: "Tasks Completed"

Task	Person(s)	Due Date	Status (Pending, Completed)
Update all accountability and benchmarking tools.			
Continue with "Communications Sequence" (items 7–10).			
Draft "Case for Support," focusing on the finalization of narrative, and begin layout.			
Discuss printing of "Case for Support" and collateral materials ("Letter of Intent").			
Schedule Church Board meeting and prepare presentation—provide update to Church Board and discuss importance of 100 percent participation by Church Board membership.			
Update and disseminate to Church Board campaign finance reports.			
Confirm strategies for awareness and promotion and implementation, including church-wide presentation.			
Revise the planned giving presentation.			

Planning, Prospect Research, Cultivation, and Solicitation

Task	Person(s)	Due Date	Status (Pending, Completed)
Schedule and confirm time and location of church-wide presentation.			
Confirm prospect listing and assignments (Taskforce members).			
Confirm gift receipts from co-chairs and Taskforce members.			
Confirm Month 6: "Tasks to Be Completed."			
Confirm Month 6 meeting—date, time, place, and attendance.			
Prepare Month 6 meeting materials.			
Other:			

*Other activities will be added to this list as opportunities are identified.

EXHIBIT 6-5
"Communications Sequence"

Communication	Description
Month 6	
7	Invitation to Church Board to Participate in Planned Gifts Program (Letter from Co-Chairs)
8	Invitation to Former Church Board to Participate in Planned Gifts Program (Letter from Co-Chairs)
9	Invitation to Taskforce to Participate in Planned Gifts Program (Letter from Co-Chairs)
10	Planned Giving Introduction (Bulletin)

EXHIBIT 6-11
Month 6: "Tasks to Be Completed"

Task	Person(s)	Due Date	Status (Pending, Completed)
Update all campaign accountability and benchmark forms ("Master Schedule," "Plan of Campaign," and monthly "Tasks to Be Completed").			
Acquire the printed "Case for Support."			
Disseminate Communications 7–10 according to the schedule.			
The time and location of a church-wide presentation will be determined and confirmed. The presentation should be reviewed and modified with inclusions to the campaign initiatives, leadership, and timing.			
The "Control Sheet" should be updated, which will include assignments of Taskforce co-chairs and members to prospects. A total of seventy-four individuals should be identified for solicitation purposes—two co-chairs (to be conducted by the clergy), twelve Taskforce members (to be conducted by the co-chairs), and a minimum of sixty parishioners (to be conducted by the twelve Taskforce members).			

(continued on page 100)

Task	Person(s)	Due Date	Status (Pending, Completed)
The gifts of the Taskforce members should be received.			
Confirmation of the Church Board endorsement will be acquired as well as their intent to participate in the program. "Letter of Intent" will be distributed and a deadline for submission determined.			
The scheduling of Taskforce member-prospect solicitations can be initiated.			
Confirm Month 7 meeting—date, time, place, and attendance.			
Prepare Month 7 meeting materials.			
Other:			

Other activities will be added to this list as opportunities are identified.

MONTH 7
Prospect Research, Cultivation, and Solicitation

Objectives

- Continue with campaign accountability and benchmarking processes, including use of the "Tasks to Be Completed," "Master Schedule," and "Plan of Campaign," and evaluate and adjust accordingly.
- Receive and distribute the "Case for Support."
- Delegate and confirm the master prospect list for volunteers—to include the identification of Group 1 prospects and categorize remaining prospects into three additional groups.
- Continue the implementation of the awareness and cultivation program via the "Communications Sequence."
- Acquire gifts from selected volunteers and Church Board, and initiate the solicitation of prospects identified as "qualified" and included in Group 1.

Participants

- Clergy
- Church Board chair or vice chair
- Stewardship Committee chair
- Church administrator (or appointee)

- Planned Gifts Taskforce co-chairs (two)
- Planned Gifts Taskforce members (twelve)

Pre-Meeting Activities to Be Completed

- Review and update the "Master Schedule" and control sheets.
- Revise "Plan of Campaign" as deemed necessary.
- Update the Organization Chart to include any additional assignments of all prospect selections by volunteers. Identify volunteers/prospects by progress of cultivated, solicited, and pledged. Each of the "cells" for volunteers should contain three letters in each corner ("C-Cultivated; S-Solicited; P-Pledged"). This approach will show progress to gift realization. As each prospect (which is assigned to a Taskforce member) is cultivated, then the corresponding letter is circled. The same holds true for "soliciting" and "pledged" (when a "Letter of Intent" is received).
- Acquire "Letter of Intent" from all Church Board members. Send "thank-you" note within seventy-two hours of receipt of a "Letter of Intent."
- Continue implementation of the "Communications Sequence," including submission of Communications 7–10.
- Confirm Month 7 meeting—date, time, place, and attendance.
- Update the "Tasks to Be Completed" form.
- Generate all necessary materials for Month 7 meeting.

Meeting Activities to Be Completed

1. The previous month's "Tasks Completed" should be reviewed and status of each item detailed. Items that have been completed, partially completed, or not completed should be identified on the "Master Schedule" and "Plan of Campaign." Timelines for the latter two categories should be discerned for completion. The names of Taskforce members assigned to the task completion should be identified.
2. The "Communications Sequence" should be reviewed and dates of submissions detailed.

3. Each Taskforce member will confirm their selections of five to six prospects (parishioners). The prospects will be prioritized with the most "qualified" prospects (Group 1) to be solicited during the next three to four weeks. The remaining four to five prospects that each Taskforce member has selected will be placed into three additional groups—based upon most likely to participate in the planned gifts program to least likely. The groupings will serve as the basis for solicitation for the remaining conduct of the campaign.

4. During the course of the meeting, an update on solicitations to date should occur, including receipt of all "Letters of Intent" and expressions of interest (Church Board). A schedule for prospect solicitations (Group 1) can be initiated by all Taskforce members; however, no solicitations should occur until attainment of the "Case for Support." If the "Case for Support" is available, each member of the Taskforce should receive ample copies necessary (including the "Letter of Intent") for the conduct of six solicitations.

5. Specific tasks will be delineated. Individuals responsible for the completion of the activities as well as associated dates will be determined.

Post-Meeting Activities to Be Completed

- Update all campaign accountability and benchmark forms ("Master Schedule," "Plan of Campaign," and monthly "Tasks to Be Completed").
- Distribute the printed "Case for Support" as needed.
- Communications 11, 12, and 13 should be revised and disseminated according to the schedule.
- All remaining (outstanding) Church Board member "Letters of Intent" should be obtained prior to Month 8 meeting.
- Each Taskforce member should immediately begin the scheduling of prospect solicitations with prospects that have been categorized in Group 1. Sufficient solicitation materials, including "Cases for Support" and "Letters of Intent," should be provided to each Taskforce member (one set for each "qualified" prospect in Group 1).
- The solicitations of all Group 1 prospects should be initiated and conducted before the Month 8 meeting (approximately four weeks).

Solicitation updates should be provided to the Taskforce co-chairs and/or the church office.

- Confirm Month 8 meeting—date, time, place, and attendance.
- Update the "Tasks to Be Completed" form.
- Generate all necessary materials for Month 8 meeting.

Exhibits

- Organizational Meeting Agenda: Month 7 (Exhibit 7-1)
- Month 7—Prayer (Exhibit 7-2)
- Month 6: "Tasks Completed" (Exhibit 7-3)
- "Communications Sequence" (Exhibit 7-4)
- Communication 11—Information on "Ways to Give—Insurance" (Bulletin) (Exhibit 7-5)*
- Communication 12—Information on "Ways to Give—Bequests" (Bulletin) (Exhibit 7-6)*
- Communication 13—Information on "Ways to Give—Trusts" (Bulletin) (Exhibit 7-7)*
- Prospect Identification and Research (Exhibit 7-8)
- Month 7: "Tasks to Be Completed" (Exhibit 7-9)

EXHIBIT 7-1
Organizational Meeting Agenda: Month 7 (one hour)

- Welcome and overview
- Prayer (Exhibit 7-2)
- Campaign progress:
  - Review Month 6: "Tasks Completed" (Exhibit 7-3).
  - "Master Schedule" (page 3)
  - "Plan of Campaign" (page 5)
- "Case for Support" and collateral materials
- "Communications Sequence" (Exhibit 7-4):
  - Communication 11—Information on "Ways to Give—Insurance" (Bulletin) (Exhibit 7-5)*
  - Communication 12—Information on "Ways to Give—Bequests" (Bulletin) (Exhibit 7-6)*
  - Communication 13—Information on "Ways to Give—Trusts" (Bulletin) (Exhibit 7-7)*
- Prospect Identification and Research (Exhibit 7-8)
- Solicitation update (page 17):
  - Taskforce members
  - Church Board/former Church Board
  - Group 1
- Review Month 7: "Tasks to Be Completed" (Exhibit 7-9).
- Schedule of next meeting.
- Adjournment

EXHIBIT 7-2
Month 7—Prayer

O Lord God, our Father, Savior, and Comforter, we are reminded, from time to time, about our duty as Christians to make prudent provisions for the well-being of our families, and for all persons to make wills, while they are in health, arranging for the disposal of their temporal goods, not neglecting, if they are able to leave bequests for their church and its ministries. Enable those of us who are making this duty known to our fellow Christians to fulfill your will; in Christ's name we pray.

   Amen

(BCP, page 445)

EXHIBIT 7-3
Month 6: "Tasks Completed"

Task	Person(s)	Due Date	Status (Pending, Completed)
Update all campaign accountability and benchmark forms ("Master Schedule," "Plan of Campaign," and monthly "Tasks to Be Completed").			
Acquire and distribute the printed "Case for Support."			
Communications 1–13 are drafted.			
The time and location of a church-wide presentation will be determined and confirmed. The presentation should be reviewed and modified with inclusions to the campaign initiatives, leadership, and timing.			
The "Control Sheet" should be updated, which will include assignments of Taskforce co-chairs and members to prospects. A total of seventy-four individuals should be identified for solicitation purposes—two co-chairs (to be conducted by the clergy), twelve Taskforce members (to be conducted by the co-chairs), and a minimum of sixty parishioners (to be conducted by the twelve Taskforce members).			

(continued on page 108)

Task	Person(s)	Due Date	Status (Pending, Completed)
The gifts of the Taskforce members should be received.			
Confirmation of the Church Board endorsement will be acquired as well as their intent to participate in the program. "Letter of Intent" will be distributed and a deadline for submission determined.			
The scheduling of Taskforce member-prospect solicitations can be initiated.			
Confirm Month 7 meeting—date, time, place, and attendance.			
Prepare Month 7 meeting materials.			
Other:			

*Other activities will be added to this list as opportunities are identified.

EXHIBIT 7-4
"Communications Sequence"

Communication	Description
Month 7	
11	Information on "Ways to Give—Insurance" (Bulletin)
12	Information on "Ways to Give—Bequests" (Bulletin)
13	Information on "Ways to Give—Trusts" (Bulletin)

EXHIBIT 7-8
Prospect Identification and Research

At this juncture in the process, the initiation of parishioner solicitation should begin. As noted in the "Planned Giving Fundamentals," a direct solicitation is recommended—including a face-to-face meeting. As such, the outcome of the "ask" is dependent upon a number of factors. First, how well informed is the prospect of what is attempting to be done? Second, what is the extent of change that will be made (will the effort really make a measurable difference in the way that the church will conduct business and advance spirituality)? Third, is the relationship between volunteer and prospect significant?

The answers to the first two questions should not be an issue at this point in the campaign. The third question is one that should be reaffirmed. Currently, each volunteer has identified five to six prospects and has listed their names on the Organization Chart. Now:

- The prospects should be prioritized from the "easiest" one (for the purposes of solicitation) to the most challenging one.
- A prescribed approach that embodies uniqueness, personal interests, and circumstances should be considered—based upon the knowledge that the volunteer has on the prospect.
- Then, each of the five to six prospects should be assigned into one of four groupings based upon the relationship criteria and judgments made above.

The goal at this point is to begin the solicitation process focusing on the "easiest" prospect first. Further, there should be a solicitation scheduled, conducted, and finalized once every two to three weeks.

Each of the volunteers will conduct this strategy. The result will be an assembly of names that are more likely to participate early on in the process, which will: (a) establish a level of momentum in the campaign—thus, creating a sense of credibility and enthusiasm; (b) further break down a significant body of work into smaller units that can be measured and completed in a timely manner; and (c) realize and enjoy success on a month-by-month basis.

EXHIBIT 7-9
Month 7: "Tasks to Be Completed"

Task	Person(s)	Due Date	Status (Pending, Completed)
Update all campaign accountability and benchmark forms ("Master Schedule," "Plan of Campaign," and monthly "Tasks to Be Completed").			
Distribute the printed "Case for Support."			
Communications 11, 12, and 13 should be revised and disseminated according to the schedule.			
The "Control Sheet" should be updated, which will include assignments of Taskforce co-chairs and members to prospects and detail updates on cultivation, solicitation, and pledges—for Group 1.			
The gifts of Group 1 should be solicited.			
The scheduling of Taskforce member-prospect solicitations should continue for Group 2.			
Confirm Month 8 meeting—date, time, place, and attendance.			

(continued on page 112)

Task	Person(s)	Due Date	Status (Pending, Completed)
Prepare Month 8 meeting materials.			
Stewardship activities should be initiated.			
Other:			

*Other activities will be added to this list as opportunities are identified.

MONTH 8
Prospect Research, Cultivation, and Solicitation

Objectives

- Continue with campaign accountability and benchmarking processes, including use of the "Tasks to Be Completed," "Master Schedule," and "Plan of Campaign," and evaluate and adjust accordingly.
- Distribute any additional "Cases for Support," if deemed necessary.
- Delegate and confirm the master prospect list for volunteers—to include the identification of Group 1 and 2 prospects and categorize remaining prospects into two additional groups.
- Continue the implementation of the awareness and cultivation program via the "Communications Sequence."
- Acquire gifts from selected volunteers and Church Board, and initiate the solicitation of prospects identified as "qualified" and included in Groups 1 and 2.
- Conduct initial planning of the stewardship and celebration.

Participants

- Clergy
- Church Board chair or vice chair
- Stewardship Committee chair
- Church administrator (or appointee)
- Planned Gifts Taskforce co-chairs (two)
- Planned Gifts Taskforce members (twelve)

Pre-Meeting Activities to Be Completed

- Review and update the "Master Schedule," "Tasks Completed," and control sheets.
- Revise "Plan of Campaign" as deemed necessary.
- Update the Organization Chart to include volunteers/prospects' progress of cultivated, solicited, and pledged ("C-Cultivated; S-Solicited; P-Pledged"). Further, each of the prospects has now been categorized into a total of four groups—distinguishing order of solicitation (1–4). The names included in Group 1 should have all been cultivated and solicited at this point. The goal is to acquire 100 percent of the Group 1 prospects before the monthly meeting. In addition, the second meeting of the solicitation meeting for Group 1 prospects should be scheduled and occur as soon as possible—along with solicitation meetings for parishioners in Group 2, which would be the initial solicitation visit.
- Acquire all remaining "Letters of Intent" from all Church Board members. Send "thank-you" note within seventy-two hours of receipt of a "Letter of Intent."
- Continue implementation of the "Communications Sequence," including drafting Communications 14 and 15.
- Confirm Month 8 meeting—date, time, place, and attendance.
- Update the "Tasks to Be Completed" form.
- Generate all necessary materials for Month 8 meeting.

Meeting Activities to Be Completed

- The previous month's "Tasks Completed" should be reviewed and status of each item detailed. Items that have been completed, partially completed, or not completed should be identified on the "Master Schedule" and "Plan of Campaign." Timelines for the latter two categories should be discerned for completion. The names of Taskforce members assigned to the task completion should be identified.

- The "Communications Sequence" should be reviewed and dates of submissions detailed. The final version of Communications 14 and 15 should be completed and scheduled for dissemination.

- Each Taskforce member will confirm status for each of their four solicitation groups. A goal of 100 percent gift acquisition for all Group 1 prospects should be realized. The prospects associated with Group 2 will now be confirmed at the meeting and solicitation processes and timing discussed. The goal is to solicit all parishioners associated with Group 2 during the next three to four weeks.

- At this point in the process, there are approximately four months remaining. As such, initial discussion of stewardship should occur. It is recommended that three processes be employed to "steward" all donors. First, within seventy-two hours of the gift receipt, each member should receive a handwritten "thank-you" note. Further, information on the development of a plaque should be acquired—which would include the names of all founding members of the "Society." Finally, a banquet for all participants during Month 12 should be confirmed.

- Specific tasks will be delineated. Individuals responsible for the completion of the activities as well as associated dates will be determined.

Post-Meeting Activities to Be Completed

- Update all campaign accountability and benchmark forms ("Master Schedule," "Plan of Campaign," and monthly "Tasks to Be Completed").
- Communications 14 and 15 should be revised and disseminated according to the schedule.
- Sufficient solicitation materials, including "Cases for Support" and "Letters of Intent," should be provided to each Taskforce member (one set for each "qualified" prospect in Group 2 as well as all remaining solicitation Groups 3–4).
- The solicitations of all Group 2 prospects should be initiated and conducted before the Month 9 meeting (approximately four weeks). Solicitation updates should be provided to the Taskforce co-chairs and/or the church office. All remaining (outstanding) Group 2 "Letters of Intent" should be obtained prior to Month 9 meeting.
- All three of the stewardship activities should occur, including "thank-you" notes, research on materials and costs of the plaque, and the scheduling and costs of the banquet. It should be noted that the plaque will be displayed in a location that is visible and prominent. The banquet would be off-site and in a location where a series of presentations can be made.
- Confirm Month 9 meeting—date, time, place, and attendance.
- Update the "Tasks to Be Completed" form.
- Generate all necessary materials for Month 9 meeting.

Exhibits

- Organizational Meeting Agenda: Month 8 (Exhibit 8-1)
- Month 8—Prayer (Exhibit 8-2)
- Month 7: "Tasks Completed" (Exhibit 8-3)
- "Communications Sequence" (Exhibit 8-4)
- Communication 14—Planned Giving Update (Bulletin) (Exhibit 8-5)*
- Communication 15—Planned Giving Testimonial (Bulletin) (Exhibit 8-6)*
- Prospect Identification and Research (Exhibit 8-7)
- Month 8: "Tasks to Be Completed" (Exhibit 8-8)

EXHIBIT 8-1

Organizational Meeting Agenda: Month 8 (one hour)

- Welcome and overview
- Prayer (Exhibit 8-2)
- Campaign progress:
  - Review Month 7: "Tasks Completed" (Exhibit 8-3).
  - "Master Schedule" (page 3)
  - "Plan of Campaign" (page 5)
- "Case for Support" and collateral materials
- "Communications Sequence" (Exhibit 8-4):
  - Communication 14—Planned Giving Update (Bulletin) (Exhibit 8-5)*
  - Communication 15—Planned Giving Testimonial (Bulletin) (Exhibit 8-6)*
- Prospect Identification and Research (Exhibit 8-7)
- Solicitation update (page 17):
  - Taskforce members
  - Church Board/former Church Board
  - Group 1
  - Group 2
- Review Month 8: "Tasks to Be Completed" (Exhibit 8-8).
- Schedule next meeting.
- Adjournment

EXHIBIT 8-2
Month 8—Prayer

Almighty God, whose loving hand has given us all that we possess: Grant us grace that we may honor you with our substance, and that we, remembering the account that we must one day give, may be faithful stewards of your bounty; through Jesus Christ our Lord.
    Amen

(BCP, page 827)

EXHIBIT 8-3
Month 7: "Tasks Completed"

Task	Person(s)	Due Date	Status (Pending, Completed)
Update all campaign accountability and benchmark forms ("Master Schedule," "Plan of Campaign," and monthly "Tasks to Be Completed").			
Distribute the printed "Case for Support."			
Communications 14 and 15 should be drafted and approved.			
The "Control Sheet" should be updated, which will include assignments of Taskforce co-chairs and members to prospects and detail updates on cultivation, solicitation, and pledges—for Group 1.			
The gifts of Group 1 should be solicited.			
The scheduling of Taskforce member-prospect solicitations should continue for Group 2.			
Confirm Month 8 meeting—date, time, place, and attendance.			
Prepare Month 8 meeting materials.			

Task	Person(s)	Due Date	Status (Pending, Completed)
Stewardship activities should be initiated.			
Other:			

*Other activities will be added to this list as opportunities are identified.

EXHIBIT 8-4
"Communications Sequence"

Communication	Description
Month 8	
14	Planned Giving Update (Bulletin)
15	Planned Giving Testimonial (Bulletin)

EXHIBIT 8-7
Prospect Identification and Research

At this juncture in the process, the initiation of parishioner solicitation should begin. As noted in the "Planned Giving Fundamentals," a direct solicitation is recommended—including a face-to-face meeting. As such, the outcome of the "ask" is dependent upon a number of factors. First, how well informed is the prospect of what is attempting to be done? Secondly, what is the extent of change that will be made (will the effort really make a measurable difference in the way that the church will conduct business and advance spirituality)? Thirdly, is the relationship between volunteer and prospect significant?

The answers to the first two questions should not be an issue at this point in the campaign. The third question is one that should be reaffirmed. Currently, each volunteer has identified five to six prospects and has listed their names on the Organization Chart. Now:

- The prospects should be prioritized from the "easiest" one (for the purposes of solicitation) to the most challenging one.
- A prescribed approach that embodies uniqueness, personal interests, and circumstances should be considered—based upon the knowledge that the volunteer has on the prospect.
- Then, each of the five to six prospects should be assigned into one of four groupings based upon the relationship criteria and judgments made above.

The goal at this point is to begin the solicitation process focusing on the "easiest" prospect first. Further, there should be a solicitation scheduled, conducted, and finalized once every two to three weeks.

Each of the volunteers will conduct this strategy. The result will be an assembly of names that are more likely to participate early on in the process, which will: (a) establish a level of momentum in the campaign—thus, creating a sense of credibility and enthusiasm; (b) further break down a significant body of work into smaller units that can be measured and completed in a timely manner; and (c) realize and enjoy success on a month-by-month basis.

EXHIBIT 8-8
Month 8: "Tasks to Be Completed"

Task	Person(s)	Due Date	Status (Pending, Completed)
Update all campaign accountability and benchmark forms ("Master Schedule," "Plan of Campaign," and monthly "Tasks to Be Completed").			
Distribute the printed "Case for Support."			
Communications 14 and 15 should be disseminated according to the schedule.			
Solicitation materials should be provided to each Taskforce member for all qualified prospects in Groups 2, 3, and 4.			
All Group 1 "Letters of Intent" should be received.			
Solicitation for all Group 2 prospects should be initiated.			
Thank-you notes, research on the plaque, and scheduling of banquet should be completed.			
Confirm Month 9 meeting—date, time, place, and attendance.			

Task	Person(s)	Due Date	Status (Pending, Completed)
Prepare Month 9 meeting materials.			
Stewardship activities should be initiated.			
Other:			

*Other activities will be added to this list as opportunities are identified.

MONTH 9
Prospect Research, Cultivation, and Solicitation

Objectives

- Continue with campaign accountability and benchmarking processes, including use of the "Tasks Completed," "Master Schedule," and "Plan of Campaign," and evaluate and adjust accordingly.
- Continue to distribute the "Case for Support" to volunteers.
- Delegate and confirm the master prospect list for volunteers—to include the identification of Group 3 prospects and categorize remaining prospects into three additional groups.
- Continue the implementation of the awareness and cultivation program via the "Communications Sequence."
- Acquire gifts from Groups 1 and 2 and initiate the solicitation of prospects identified as "qualified" and included in Group 3.
- Continue planning of the stewardship and celebration.

Participants

- Clergy
- Church Board chair or vice chair
- Stewardship Committee chair
- Church administrator (or appointee)
- Planned Gifts Taskforce co-chairs (two)
- Planned Gifts Taskforce members (twelve)

Pre-Meeting Activities to Be Completed

- Review and update the "Master Schedule," "Tasks Completed," and control sheets.
- Revise "Plan of Campaign" as deemed necessary.
- Review the Organization Chart to include volunteers/prospects' progress of cultivated, solicited, and pledged ("C-Cultivated; S-Solicited; P-Pledged"). The names included in Groups 1 and 2 should have all been cultivated and solicited at this point. It is common to have some gifts secured (with "Letter of Intent" acquired). A realistic goal is to acquire 100 percent of the Group 1 prospects and approximately 50 percent of Group 2 before the monthly meeting. In addition, the second meeting, as distinguished in the solicitation process for Group 2 prospects, should be scheduled and occur as soon as possible—along with solicitation meetings for parishioners in Group 3, which would be the initial solicitation meeting—as described in the process.
- Acquire all remaining "Letters of Intent" from all Group 1 members. Send "thank-you" note within seventy-two hours of receipt of a "Letter of Intent."
- Continue implementation of the "Communications Sequence," including submission of Communications 14 and 15. Draft Communications 16, 17, and 18.
- Confirm Month 9 meeting—date, time, place, and attendance.
- Update the "Tasks Completed" form.
- Generate all necessary materials for Month 9 meeting.

Meeting Activities to Be Completed

- The previous month's "Tasks Completed" should be reviewed and status of each item detailed. Items that have been completed, partially completed, or not completed should be identified on the "Master Schedule" and "Plan of Campaign." Timelines for the latter two categories should be discerned for completion. The names of Taskforce members assigned to the task completion should be identified.
- The "Communications Sequence" should be reviewed and dates of submissions detailed. The final version of Communications 16, 17, and 18 should be completed and scheduled for dissemination.
- Each Taskforce member will confirm status for each of their four solicitation groups. A goal of 100 percent gift acquisition for all Group 1 prospects should be realized. Gift realization for 50 percent of Group 2 prospects should be acquired. Specific processes should be discussed on all prospects that have been through the solicitation process but have yet to submit a "Letter of Intent." The prospects associated with Group 3 will now be confirmed at the meeting and solicitation processes and timing discussed. The goal is to solicit all parishioners associated with Group 3 during the next three to four weeks.
- At this point in the process, there are approximately three months remaining. As such, initial discussion of stewardship should occur. It is recommended that three processes be employed to "steward" all donors. First, within seventy-two hours of the gift receipt, each member should receive a handwritten "thank-you" note. Further, information obtained on the development of a plaque should be discussed and details finalized—which would include the names of all founding members of the "Society." Finally, a banquet for all participants during Month 12 should be confirmed—in terms of costs per attendee, location, and date and time.
- Specific tasks will be delineated. Individuals responsible for the completion of the activities as well as associated dates will be determined.

Post-Meeting Activities to Be Completed

- Update all campaign accountability and benchmark forms ("Master Schedule," "Plan of Campaign," and monthly "Tasks to Be Completed").
- Disseminate additional "Cases for Support," if deemed necessary.
- Communications 16, 17, and 18 should be revised and disseminated according to the schedule.
- All remaining (outstanding) Group 1 and 2 "Letters of Intent" should be obtained prior to Month 10 meeting. Approximately 50 percent of Group 3 Letters should be acquired.
- The solicitations of all Group 3 prospects should be initiated and conducted before the Month 10 meeting (approximately four weeks). Solicitation updates should be provided to the Taskforce co-chairs and/or the church office.
- All three of the stewardship activities should occur, including "thank-you" notes, research on materials and costs of the plaque, and the scheduling and costs of the banquet. The time and date of the banquet should be confirmed. The invitation to the banquet should be drafted and readied for the Month 10 meeting. Specific information and details on the plaque should be confirmed.
- Confirm Month 10 meeting—date, time, place, and attendance.
- Update the "Tasks to Be Completed" form.
- Generate all necessary materials for Month 10 meeting.

Exhibits

- Organizational Meeting Agenda: Month 9 (Exhibit 9-1)
- Month 9—Prayer (Exhibit 9-2)
- Month 8: "Tasks Completed" (Exhibit 9-3)
- "Communications Sequence" (Exhibit 9-4)
- Communication 16—Planned Giving Update (Bulletin) (Exhibit 9-5)*
- Communication 17—Planned Giving Update (Service Announcement) (Exhibit 9-6)*
- Communication 18—Planned Giving Update to All Parishioners (Letter) (Exhibit 9-7)*
- Prospect Identification and Research (Exhibit 9-8)
- Month 9: "Tasks to Be Completed" (9-9)

EXHIBIT 9-1

Organizational Meeting Agenda: Month 9 (one hour)

- Welcome and overview
- Prayer (Exhibit 9-2)
- Campaign progress:
  - Review Month 8: "Tasks Completed" (Exhibit 9-3).
  - "Master Schedule" (page 3)
  - "Plan of Campaign" (page 5)
- "Communications Sequence" (Exhibit 9-4):
  - Communication 19—Planned Giving Update (Bulletin) (Exhibit 9-5)*
  - Communication 20—Planned Giving Update (Service Announcement) (Exhibit 9-6)*
  - Communication 21—Planned Giving Update to All Parishioners (Letter) (Exhibit 9-7)*
- Prospect Identification and Research (Exhibit 9-8)
- Solicitation update (page 17):
  - Taskforce members
  - Church Board/former Church Board
  - Group 1
  - Group 2
  - Group 3
- Review Month 9: "Tasks to Be Completed" (Exhibit 9-9).
- Schedule next meeting.
- Adjournment

EXHIBIT 9-2
Month 9—Prayer

Lord of our lives, teach us to use rightly our money and all our possessions. Deliver us from meanness or extravagance; may the spirit of true generosity inspire our giving. In all our getting and our spending, keep us ever mindful of your generous love, that we may be wise and faithful stewards of the good gifts you have given us; for your mercy's sake.
 Amen

EXHIBIT 9-3
Month 8: "Tasks Completed"

Task	Person(s)	Due Date	Status (Pending, Completed)
Update all campaign accountability and benchmark forms ("Master Schedule," "Plan of Campaign," and monthly "Tasks to Be Completed").			
Distribute the printed "Case for Support."			
Communications 19, 20, and 21 should be revised.			
Solicitation materials should be provided to each Taskforce member for all qualified prospects in Groups 2, 3, and 4.			
All Group 1 "Letters of Intent" should be received.			
Solicitation for all Group 2 prospects should be initiated.			
Thank-you notes, research on the plaque, and scheduling of banquet should be completed.			
Confirm Month 9 meeting—date, time, place, and attendance.			
Prepare Month 9 meeting materials.			

Task	Person(s)	Due Date	Status (Pending, Completed)
Stewardship activities should be initiated.			
Other:			

*Other activities will be added to this list as opportunities are identified.

EXHIBIT 9-4
"Communications Sequence"

Communication	Description
Month 9	
16	Planned Giving Update (Bulletin)
17	Planned Giving Update (Service Announcement)
18	Planned Giving Update to All Parishioners (Letter)

EXHIBIT 9-8
Prospect Identification and Research

At this juncture in the process, the initiation of parishioner solicitation should begin. As noted in the "Planned Giving Fundamentals," a direct solicitation is recommended—including a face-to-face meeting. As such, the outcome of the "ask" is dependent upon a number of factors. First, how well informed is the prospect of what is attempting to be done? Second, what is the extent of change that will be made (will the effort really make a measurable difference in the way that the church will conduct business and advance spirituality)? Third, is the relationship between volunteer and prospect significant?

The answers to the first two questions should not be an issue at this point in the campaign. The third question is one that should be reaffirmed. Currently, each volunteer has identified five to six prospects and have listed their names on the Organization Chart. Now:

- The prospects should be prioritized from the "easiest" one (for the purposes of solicitation) to the most challenging one.
- A prescribed approach that embodies uniqueness, personal interests, and circumstances should be considered—based upon the knowledge that the volunteer has on the prospect.
- Then, each of the five to six prospects should be assigned to one of four groupings based upon the relationship criteria and judgments made above.

The goal at this point is to begin the solicitation process focusing on the "easiest" prospect first. Further, there should be a solicitation scheduled, conducted, and finalized once every two to three weeks.

Each of the volunteers will conduct this strategy. The result will be an assembly of names that are more likely to participate early on in the process, which will: (a) establish a level of momentum in the campaign—thus, creating a sense of credibility and enthusiasm; (b) further break down a significant body of work into smaller units that can be measured and completed in a timely manner; and (c) realize and enjoy success on a month-by-month basis.

EXHIBIT 9-9
Month 9: "Tasks to Be Completed"

Task	Person(s)	Due Date	Status (Pending, Completed)
Update all campaign accountability and benchmark forms ("Master Schedule," "Plan of Campaign," and monthly "Tasks to Be Completed").			
Distribute the printed "Case for Support."			
Communications 8, 9, and 10 should be revised and disseminated according to the schedule.			
The "Control Sheet" should be updated, which will include assignments of Taskforce co-chairs and members to prospects and detail updates on cultivation, solicitation, and pledges—for Group 1.			
The gifts of Group 1 should be received.			
The scheduling of Taskforce member-prospect solicitations should continue for Group 2.			
Confirm Month 10 meeting—date, time, place, and attendance.			

Task	Person(s)	Due Date	Status (Pending, Completed)
Prepare Month 10 meeting materials.			
Stewardship activities should be initiated.			
Other:			

*Other activities will be added to this list as opportunities are identified.

MONTH 10
Prospect Research, Cultivation, and Solicitation

Objectives

- Continue with campaign accountability and benchmarking processes, including use of the "Tasks Completed," "Master Schedule," and "Plan of Campaign," and evaluate and adjust accordingly.
- Continue to distribute the "Case for Support" to volunteers and parishioners.
- Delegate and confirm the master prospect list for volunteers—to include the identification of Group 3 prospects and categorize remaining prospects into three additional groups.
- Continue the implementation of the awareness and cultivation program via the "Communications Sequence."
- Acquire 100 percent of gifts from Groups 1 and 2 and approximately 50 percent of prospect gifts associated with Group 3.
- Initiate the solicitation of prospects identified as "qualified" and included in Group 4.
- Finalize planning of the stewardship and celebration.

Participants

- Clergy
- Church Board chair or vice chair
- Stewardship Committee chair
- Church administrator (or appointee)
- Planned Gifts Taskforce co-chairs (two)
- Planned Gifts Taskforce members (twelve)

Pre-Meeting Activities to Be Completed

- Review and update the "Master Schedule," "Tasks Completed," and control sheets.
- Revise "Plan of Campaign" as deemed necessary.
- Review the Organization Chart to include volunteers/prospects' progress of cultivated, solicited, and pledged ("C-Cultivated; S-Solicited; P-Pledged"). The names included in Groups 1 and 2 should have all been cultivated and solicited at this point. It is common to have some gifts secured (with "Letter of Intent" acquired). A realistic goal is to acquire 100 percent of the Group 1 and 2 prospects and approximately 50 percent of Group 3 before the monthly meeting. In addition, the second solicitation meeting, as distinguished in the solicitation process for Group 3 remaining prospects, should be scheduled and occur as soon as possible—along with solicitation meetings for parishioners in Group 4, which would be the initial solicitation meeting—as described in the process.
- Acquire all remaining "Letters of Intent" from all Group 1 and 2 members. Send "thank-you" note within seventy-two hours of receipt of a "Letter of Intent."
- Continue implementation of the "Communications Sequence," including submission of Communications 19, 20, and 21.
- Confirm Month 10 meeting—date, time, place, and attendance.
- Update the "Tasks Completed" form.
- Generate all necessary materials for Month 10 meeting.

Meeting Activities to Be Completed

- The previous month's "Tasks Completed" should be reviewed and status of each item detailed. Items that have been completed, partially completed, or not completed should be identified on the "Master Schedule" and "Plan of Campaign." Timelines for the latter two categories should be discerned for completion. The names of Taskforce members assigned to the task completion should be identified and final dates of completion identified.
- The "Communications Sequence" should be reviewed and dates of submissions detailed. The final versions of Communications 19, 20, and 21 should be completed and scheduled for dissemination.
- Each Taskforce member will confirm status for each of their four solicitation groups. A goal of 100 percent gift acquisition for all Group 1 and 2 prospects should be realized. Gift realization for 50 percent of Group 3 prospects should be acquired. Specific processes should be discussed on all prospects that have been through the solicitation process but have yet to submit a "Letter of Intent." The prospects associated with Group 4 will now be confirmed at the meeting and solicitation processes and timing discussed. The goal is to solicit all parishioners associated with Group 4 during the next three to four weeks.
- At this point in the process, there are approximately two months remaining. As such, initial discussion of stewardship should occur. It is recommended that three processes be employed to "steward" all donors. First, within seventy-two hours of the gift receipt, each member should receive a handwritten "thank-you" note. Further, information obtained on the development of a plaque should be finalized—which would include the names of all founding members of the "Society." Finally, a banquet for all participants during Month 12 should be confirmed—in terms of costs per attendee, location, and date and time. The date of the banquet will be acknowledged and all parishioners will be notified. This information will be used as leverage as a means of securing any "Letters of Intent" from outstanding parishioners associated in any of the four groups.
- Specific tasks will be delineated. Individuals responsible for the completion of the activities as well as associated dates will be determined.

Post-Meeting Activities to Be Completed

- Update all campaign accountability and benchmark forms ("Master Schedule," "Plan of Campaign," and monthly "Tasks to Be Completed").
- All remaining (outstanding) Group 1, 2, and 3 "Letters of Intent" should be obtained prior to Month 11 meeting. Approximately 50 percent of Group 4 Letters should be acquired.
- The solicitations of all Group 4 prospects should be initiated and conducted before the Month 11 meeting (approximately four weeks). Solicitation updates should be provided to the Taskforce co-chairs and/or the church office.
- All three of the stewardship activities should continue, including "thank-you" notes, layout of the plaque, and the time and date of the banquet should be confirmed. The invitation to the banquet should be finalized and sent to the printer. Specific information and details on the plaque should be confirmed. The specifics of the banquet should be discussed in terms of presentations. If a person from "outside" of the church family is desired, then identification and confirmation of that individual should occur.
- Confirm Month 11 meeting—date, time, place, and attendance.
- Update the "Tasks to Be Completed" form.
- Generate all necessary materials for Month 11 meeting.

Exhibits

- Organizational Meeting Agenda: Month 10 (Exhibit 10-1)
- Month 10—Prayer (Exhibit 10-2)
- Month 9: "Tasks Completed" (Exhibit 10-3)
- "Communications Sequence" (Exhibit 10-4)
- Communication 19—What Our Church Means to Me (Bulletin) (Exhibit 10-5)*
- Communication 20—Planned Giving Appeal (Church Mailing) (Exhibit 10-6)*
- Communication 21—Thank You (Letter) (Exhibit 10-7)*
- Prospect Identification and Research (Exhibit 10-8)
- Month 10: "Tasks to Be Completed" (Exhibit 10-9)

EXHIBIT 10-1

Organizational Meeting Agenda: Month 10 (one hour)

- Welcome and overview
- Prayer (Exhibit 10-2)
- Campaign progress:
  - Review Month 9: "Tasks Completed" (Exhibit 10-3).
  - "Master Schedule" (page 3)
  - "Plan of Campaign" (page 5)
- "Communications Sequence" (Exhibit 10-4):
  - Communication 19—What Our Church Means to Me (Bulletin) (Exhibit 10-5)*
  - Communication 20—Planned Giving Appeal (Church Mailing) (Exhibit 10-6)*
  - Communication 21—Thank You (Letter) (Exhibit 10-7)*
- Prospect Identification and Research (Exhibit 10-8)
- Solicitation update (page 17):
  - Taskforce members
  - Church Board/former Church Board
  - Group 1
  - Group 2
  - Group 3
  - Group 4
- Review Month 10: "Tasks to Be Completed" (Exhibit 10-9).
- Schedule next meeting.
- Adjournment

EXHIBIT 10-2

Month 10—Prayer

Almighty God, who orders all things and has called us to your service: Enable us to use wisely the time, ability, and possessions entrusted to us, that we may be good and faithful servants, and may enter at last into the joy of our Lord; through the name of our Savior Jesus Christ.

Amen

EXHIBIT 10-3
Month 9: "Tasks Completed"

Task	Person(s)	Due Date	Status (Pending, Completed)
Update all campaign accountability and benchmark forms ("Master Schedule," "Plan of Campaign," and "Tasks to Be Completed").			
Distribute the printed "Case for Support."			
Communications 16, 17, and 18 should be drafted.			
The "Control Sheet" should be updated, which will include assignments of Taskforce co-chairs and members to prospects and detail updates on cultivation, solicitation, and pledges—for Group 1.			
The gifts of Group 1 should be received.			
The scheduling of Taskforce member-prospect solicitations should continue for Group 2.			
Confirm Month10 meeting—date, time, place, and attendance.			
Prepare Month 10 meeting materials.			

Task	Person(s)	Due Date	Status (Pending, Completed)
Stewardship activities should be initiated.			
Other:			

*Other activities will be added to this list as opportunities are identified.

EXHIBIT 10-4
"Communications Sequence"

Communication	Description
Month 10	
19	What Our Church Means to Me (Bulletin)
20	Planned Giving Appeal (Church Mailing)
21	Thank You (Letter)

EXHIBIT 10-8
Prospect Identification and Research

At this juncture in the process, the initiation of parishioner solicitation should begin. As noted in the "Planned Giving Fundamentals," a direct solicitation is recommended—including a face-to-face meeting. As such, the outcome of the "ask" is dependent upon a number of factors. First, how well informed is the prospect of what is attempting to be done? Second, what is the extent of change that will be made (will the effort really make a measurable difference in the way that the church will conduct business and advance spirituality)? Third, is the relationship between volunteer and prospect significant?

The answers to the first two questions should not be an issue at this point in the campaign. The third question is one that should be reaffirmed. Currently, each volunteer has identified five to six prospects and has listed their names on the Organization Chart. Now:

- The prospects should be prioritized from the "easiest" one (for the purposes of solicitation) to the most challenging one.

- A prescribed approach that embodies uniqueness, personal interests, and circumstances should be considered—based upon the knowledge that the volunteer has on the prospect.

- Then, each of the five to six prospects should be assigned into one of four groupings based upon the relationship criteria and judgments made above.

The goal at this point is to begin the solicitation process focusing on the "easiest" prospect first. Further, there should be a solicitation scheduled, conducted, and finalized once every two to three weeks.

Each of the volunteers will conduct this strategy. The result will be an assembly of names that are more likely to participate early on in the process, which will: (a) establish a level of momentum in the campaign—thus, creating a sense of credibility and enthusiasm; (b) further break down a significant body of work into smaller units that can be measured and completed in a timely manner; and (c) realize and enjoy success on a month-by-month basis.

EXHIBIT 10-9

Month 10: "Tasks to Be Completed"

Task	Person(s)	Due Date	Status (Pending, Completed)
Hold Taskforce meeting.			
Finalize plans for continuation of planned gifts program and provide orientation to Church Board and Endowment Committee.			
Continue "Communications Sequence."			
Continue solicitation of Taskforce, Church Board, former Church Board, and members at large.			
Plan for banquet.			
Continue planning for stewardship program.			
Confirm Month 11 meeting—date, time, place, and attendance.			
Prepare Month 11 meeting materials.			
Stewardship activities should be continued.			
Other:			

*Other activities will be added to this list as opportunities are identified.

MONTH 11

Cultivation and Solicitation

Objectives

- Continue with campaign accountability and benchmarking processes, including use of the "Tasks Completed," "Master Schedule," and "Plan of Campaign," and evaluate and adjust accordingly.
- Delegate and confirm the master prospect list for volunteers—to include the update of all prospects in each of the four groups.
- Continue the implementation of the awareness and cultivation program via the "Communications Sequence."
- Acquire 100 percent of gifts from Groups 1, 2, and 3 and approximately 50 percent of prospect gifts associated with Group 4.
- Initiate the solicitation of the remaining prospects in Group 4.
- Confirm all aspects of the stewardship and celebration.

Participants

- Clergy
- Church Board chair or vice chair
- Stewardship Committee chair
- Church administrator (or appointee)
- Planned Gifts Taskforce co-chairs (two)
- Planned Gifts Taskforce members (twelve)

Pre-Meeting Activities to Be Completed

- Review and update the "Master Schedule," "Tasks Completed," and control sheets.
- Revise "Plan of Campaign" as deemed necessary.
- A realistic goal is to acquire 100 percent of the Group 1, 2, and 3 prospects and approximately 50 percent of Group 4 before the monthly meeting. In addition, the second solicitation meeting, as distinguished in the solicitation process for Group 4 remaining prospects, should be scheduled and occur as soon as possible—the closure date for the campaign should be officially announced to the congregation during the service announcements. All individuals interested in participating in the planned gifts program should have "Letters of Intent" submitted to the church office by the announced date.
- Acquire all remaining "Letters of Intent" from all Group 1, 2, and 3 members. Send "thank-you" note within seventy-two hours of receipt of a "Letter of Intent."
- Continue implementation of the "Communications Sequence," including submission of Communications 22 and 23.
- Confirm Month 11 meeting—date, time, place, and attendance
- Update the "Tasks Completed" form.
- Generate all necessary materials for Month 11 meeting.

Meeting Activities to Be Completed

- The previous month's "Tasks Completed" should be reviewed and status of each item detailed. Items that have been completed, partially completed, or not completed should be identified on the "Master Schedule" and "Plan of Campaign." Timelines for the latter two categories should be discerned for completion. The names of Taskforce members assigned to the task completion should be identified and final dates of completion identified.

- The "Communications Sequence" should be reviewed and dates of submissions detailed. The final versions of Communications 19, 20, and 21 should be completed and scheduled for dissemination.

- Each Taskforce member will confirm the status for each of their four solicitation groups. A goal of 100 percent gift acquisition for all Group 1, 2, and 3 prospects should be realized. Gift realization for 75 percent of Group 4 prospects should be planned. Specific processes should be discussed on all prospects that have been through the solicitation process but have yet to submit a "Letter of Intent." The prospects associated with Group 4 will now be confirmed at the meeting and solicitation processes and timing discussed. The goal is to solicit all parishioners associated with Group 4 during the next three to four weeks.

- At this point in the process, there are approximately two months remaining. As such, initial discussion of stewardship should occur. It is recommended that three processes be employed to "steward" all donors. First, within seventy-two hours of the gift receipt, each member should receive a handwritten "thank-you" note. Further, information obtained on the development of a plaque should be finalized—which would include the names of all founding members of the "Society." Finally, a banquet for all participants during Month 12 should be confirmed—in terms of costs per attendee, location, and date and time. The date of the banquet will be acknowledged and all parishioners will be notified. This information will be used as leverage as a means of securing any "Letters of Intent" from outstanding parishioners associated in any of the four groups.

- Specific tasks will be delineated. Individuals responsible for the completion of the activities as well as associated dates will be determined.

Post-Meeting Activities to Be Completed

- Update all campaign accountability and benchmark forms ("Master Schedule," "Plan of Campaign," and "Tasks to Be Completed").
- Communications 22 and 23 should be revised and disseminated according to the schedule.
- All remaining (outstanding) Group 1, 2, and 3 "Letters of Intent" should be obtained prior to Month 12 meeting. Approximately 75 percent of Group 4 Letters should be acquired.
- The solicitations of all Group 4 prospects should be initiated and conducted before the Month 11 meeting (approximately four weeks). Solicitation updates should be provided to the Taskforce co-chairs and/or the church office.
- All three of the stewardship activities should continue, including "thank-you notes" and layout of the plaque, and the time and date of the banquet should be confirmed. The invitation to the banquet should be finalized and sent to the printer. Specific information and details on the plaque should be confirmed. The specifics of the banquet should be discussed in terms of presentations. If a person from "outside" of the church family is desired, then identification and confirmation of that individual should occur.
- Confirm Month 12 meeting—date, time, place, and attendance.
- Update the "Tasks to Be Completed" form.
- Generate all necessary materials for Month 12 meeting.

Cultivation and Solicitation

Exhibits

- Organizational Meeting Agenda: Month 11 (Exhibit 11-1)
- Month 11—Prayer (Exhibit 11-2)
- Month 10: "Tasks Completed" (Exhibit 11-3)
- "Communications Sequence" (Exhibit 11-4)
- Communication 22—Planned Giving Evaluation (Letter) (Exhibit 11-5)*
- Communication 23—Invitation to "Planned Gifts Society" Dinner and Celebration (Mailing) (Exhibit 11-6)*
- Month 11: "Tasks to Be Completed" (Exhibit 11-7)

EXHIBIT 11-1

Organizational Meeting Agenda: Month 11 (one hour)

- Welcome and overview
- Prayer (Exhibit 11-2)
- Campaign progress:
  - Review Month 10: "Tasks Completed" (Exhibit 11-3).
  - "Master Schedule" (page 3)
  - "Plan of Campaign" (page 5)
- "Case for Support" and collateral materials
- "Communications Sequence" (Exhibit 11-4):
  - Communication 22—Planned Giving Evaluation (Exhibit 11-5)*
  - Communication 23—Invitation (Exhibit (11-6)*
- Solicitation update (page 17):
  - Taskforce members
  - Church Board/former Church Board
  - Group 1
  - Group 2
  - Group 3
  - Group 4
- Review Month 11: "Tasks to Be Completed" (Exhibit 11-7).
- Schedule next meeting.
- Adjournment

EXHIBIT 11-2

Month 11—Prayer

O God, who loves a cheerful giver, teach us by your Holy Spirit to be thoughtful and prayerful in our giving. We ask for your guidance as we are given the opportunity to plan for the future ministry at (church) and that we will be able to provide for those who follow us. Grant us the joy of the generous heart, and the spirit of love and self-sacrifice that was in Jesus Christ our Lord.
   Amen

EXHIBIT 11-3
Month 10: "Tasks Completed"

Task	Person(s)	Due Date	Status (Pending, Completed)
Hold Taskforce meeting.			
Finalize plans for continuation of planned gifts program and provide orientation to Church Board and Endowment Committee.			
Continue "Communications Sequence."			
Continue solicitation of Taskforce, Church Board, former Church Board, and members at large.			
Plan for banquet.			
Continue planning for stewardship program.			
Prepare Month 5 meeting materials.			
Stewardship activities should be continued.			
Other:			

*Other activities will be added to this list as opportunities are identified.

EXHIBIT 11-4
"Communications Sequence"

Communication	Description
Month 11	
22	Planned Giving Evaluation (Letter)
23	Invitation to "Planned Gifts Society" Dinner and Celebration (Mailing)

EXHIBIT 11-7
Month 11: "Tasks to Be Completed"

Task	Person(s)	Due Date	Status Pending/ Completed
Hold Taskforce meeting and distribute necessary materials.			
Complete final "Communications Sequence" pieces.			
Review schedule and activity.			
Review other strategies.			
Complete final preparations for banquet: time/place/preparations.			
Provide solicitation status to Church Board on: • Group 1 (twelve individuals/families) • Group 2 (twenty-four individuals/families) • Group 3 (twenty-four individuals/families) • Group 4 (twenty-four individuals/families).			
Continue solicitation of Group 3 and Group 4 prospects—presenting planned gifts proposal and "Case for Support."			
Continue solicitation of remaining prospect base—open appeal.			

Cultivation and Solicitation

Task	Person(s)	Due Date	Status Pending/ Completed
Finalize intent of segmented prospect base (Group 2).			
Confirm intent of segmented prospect base (Group 3).			
Begin solicitation of Group 4 (twenty-four individuals/families).			
Finalize open appeal (ongoing basis).			
Finalize plans for continuation of planned gifts program and provide orientation to Church Board and Endowment Committee.			
Hold banquet debriefing.			
Complete plaque submission requirements.			
Send "Society" membership communication and invitation to banquet.			
Complete gift/donor report and provide to Taskforce and Church Board.			
Update and disseminate campaign finance reports to Church Board.			
Other:			

*Other activities will be added to this list as opportunities are identified.

MONTH 12
Cultivation and Solicitation

Objectives

- Document and finalize all campaign outcomes consistent with benchmarking processes.
- Acquire 100 percent of gifts from Groups 1, 2, 3, and 4.
- Celebrate.
- Continue the planning and implementation of the stewardship program.
- Offer perceptions and ideas on program continuance.

Participants

- Clergy
- Church Board chair or vice chair
- Stewardship Committee chair
- Church administrator (or appointee)
- Planned Gifts Taskforce co-chairs (two)
- Planned Gifts Taskforce members (twelve)

Pre-Meeting Activities to Be Completed

- Review and update the "Master Schedule," "Tasks Completed," and control sheets.
- A realistic goal is to acquire 100 percent of the Group 1, 2, and 3 prospects and approximately 75 percent of Group 4 before the monthly meeting. The closure date for the campaign should be announced to the congregation for a second time during the service announcements, expressing the last appeal to individuals interested in participating in the planned gifts program. All individuals interested in participating in the planned gifts program should have "Letters of Intent" submitted to the church office by the announced date.
- Acquire all remaining "Letters of Intent" from all Group 1, 2, 3, and initial Group 4 donors. Send "thank-you" note within seventy-two hours of receipt of a "Letter of Intent."
- Continue implementation of the "Communications Sequence," including drafting and submission of Communication 24.
- Confirm Month 12 meeting—date, time, place, and attendance.
- Update the "Tasks Completed" form.
- Generate all necessary materials for Month 12 meeting.

Meeting Activities to Be Completed

- The "Communications Sequence" should be reviewed and dates of submissions detailed. The final version of Communication 24 should be completed and scheduled for dissemination.
- Each Taskforce member will confirm status for each of their four solicitation groups. A goal of 100 percent gift acquisition for all Group 1, 2, and 3 prospects should be realized. Gift realization for 75 percent of Group 4 prospects should be acquired (it should be noted that since the groups were categorized in accordance to perceived relationship, a lesser amount of gifts will be realized).
- A banquet for all participants during Month 12 should be confirmed—in terms of costs per attendee, location, and date and time. The date of the banquet will be acknowledged and all parishioners will be notified.

- Specific tasks will be delineated. Individuals responsible for the completion of the activities as well as associated dates will be determined.

Post-Meeting Activities to Be Completed

- Hold banquet and celebrate.
- Conduct any necessary follow-up.
- Announce success of the planned gifts program at the next service(s) and indicate that the program will be ongoing (with recognition banquets occurring every two years).
- Provide a campaign overview to the Church Board and incorporate the planned giving continuation processes into the annual stewardship program.

Exhibits

- Organizational Meeting Agenda: Month 12 (Exhibit 12-1)
- Month 12—Prayer (Exhibit 12-2)
- Month 11: "Tasks Completed" (Exhibit 12-3)
- "Communications Sequence" (Exhibit 12-4)
- Communication 24—Planned Giving Thank You (Letter) (Exhibit 12-5)*
- Banquet Program (Exhibit 12-6)*
- Month 12: "Tasks to Be Completed" (Exhibit 12-7)

EXHIBIT 12-1
Organizational Meeting Agenda: Month 12 (one hour)

- Welcome and overview
- Prayer (Exhibit 12-2)
- Campaign progress:
  - Review Month 11: "Tasks Completed" (Exhibit 12-3).
  - "Master Schedule" (page 3)
  - "Plan of Campaign" (page 5)
- "Communications Sequence" (Exhibit 12-4):
  - Communication 24—Planned Giving Thank You (Letter) (Exhibit 12-5)*
- Review Banquet Program (Exhibit 12-6).*
- Review Month 12: "Tasks to Be Completed" (Exhibit 12-7).
- Adjournment

EXHIBIT 12-2
Month 12—Prayer

As we conclude this year-long planning and sacrificial giving to an endowment ministry, O Lord, accept these gifts, which we will offer up to you as the token of our love and gratitude. Please grant that they may be so wisely used that by them, the work of this congregation may prosper and our kingdom enlarged.

We also lift up in thanksgiving all donors and volunteers who have given of their gifts, talents, and time. May you richly bless them for their work in this particular area of your vineyard. The overall outcome has been an expression and reaffirmation of (church) to proclaim the grace and glory of God and advance His Will.

For Christ's sake, Amen

EXHIBIT 12-3
Month 11: "Task Completed"

Task	Person(s)	Due Date	Status Pending/ Completed
Hold Taskforce meeting and distribute necessary materials.			
Complete final "Communications Sequence" pieces.			
Review schedule and activity.			
Review other strategies.			
Complete final preparations for banquet: time/place/preparations.			
Provide solicitation status to Church Board on: • Group 1 (twelve individuals/families) • Group 2 (twenty-four individuals/families) • Group 3 (twenty-four individuals/families) • Group 4 (twenty-four individuals/families).			
Continue solicitation of Group 3 and Group 4 prospects—presenting planned gifts proposal and "Case for Support."			
Continue solicitation of remaining prospect base—open appeal.			

Cultivation and Solicitation

Task	Person(s)	Due Date	Status Pending/ Completed
Finalize intent of segmented prospect base (Group 2).			
Confirm intent of segmented prospect base (Group 3).			
Begin solicitation of Group 4 (twenty-four individuals/families).			
Finalize open appeal (ongoing basis).			
Finalize plans for continuation of planned gifts program and provide orientation to Church Board and Endowment Committee.			
Hold banquet debriefing.			
Complete plaque submission requirements.			
Send "Society" membership communication and invitation to banquet.			
Complete gift/donor report and provide to Taskforce and Church Board.			
Update and disseminate campaign finance reports to Church Board.			
Other:			

*Other activities will be added to this list as opportunities are identified.

EXHIBIT 12-4
"Communications Sequence"

Communication	Description
Month 12	
24	Planned Giving Thank You (Letter)

EXHIBIT 12-7
Month 12: "Tasks to Be Completed"

Task	Person(s)	Due Date	Status (Pending, Completed)
Hold banquet and celebrate.			
Announce success of the planned gifts program at the next service(s) and indicate that the program will be ongoing (with recognition banquets occurring every two years).			
Provide a campaign overview to the Church Board and incorporate the planned giving continuation processes into the annual stewardship program.			
Conduct any necessary follow-up.			

Conclusion

Congratulations. You have successfully implemented a program that will have a lasting impact on your church's ability to advance programs and services in accordance to the will of God. Through personal sacrifice and continued stewardship, this achievement will secure resources that will enable your church to discern and resolve long-term needs—those that are planned and consistent with its strategic vision as well as those that are unforeseen at the present time. In any case, the overarching outcome of this effort is not centered upon financial gain. More importantly, it is about the ability of your church to continue its important work within and beyond its walls, which focus on advancing the church's doctrine—for generations to come. Further, through the completion of the planned gifts program, your church has realized a very important milestone in its long history of serving God.

We hope that you have witnessed:

- A renewal in commitment of faith throughout the church
- A demonstration of sacrifice
- An energy and enthusiasm throughout the church as demonstrated through service
- A greater sense of community responsibility and obligation
- A sense of fulfillment by volunteers and parishioners knowing that a significant effort in the life of their church has been achieved

It should be noted that a program of this nature does require continued stewardship. Parishioners should constantly be recognized, thereby feeling a sense of "belonging" to a special affinity within the congregation, and provided updates on the status and advancements of the program. It is recommended that some type of event be held every two years to offer special recognition of those individuals participating in the planned gifts program.

The true measure of success is the church's ability to sustain the effort. Thus, the program should be integrated into the annual planning of the stewardship calendar. Specific goals and objectives should be discerned and concentrated on the planned giving arena—as a means of maintaining the necessary momentum for the program. It is common for the church to have realized a portion of the congregation expressing a lack of interest in participation. In many instances, a "no" from a parishioner is simply a message that means "not yet." So, the opportunity of participating in the program for members of the congregation not currently doing so must continue to be expressed and made available.

However, for now it is time to thank God for instilling the wisdom, talents, and energy necessary to begin and successfully complete a significant undertaking.